The Circle of Trust

The Circle of Trust

Reflections on the Essence of Horses and Horsemanship

Walter Zettl

with Paul Schopf and Jane Seigler

Half Halt Press, Inc.
Boonsboro, Maryland

THE CIRCLE OF TRUST
Reflections on the Essence of Horses and Horsemanship

Printed in China

Half Halt Press, Inc.
P.O. Box 67
Boonsboro, MD 21713
www.halfhaltpress.com

Translation of **Reiter-Revue** article by the kind permission of the publishers.

Cover and interior design by Sara Podgur Hoffman

Indexing by Kay Meredith Dusheck

Library of Congress Cataloging-in-Publication Data

Zettl, Walter A.
  The circle of trust : reflections on the essence of horses and horse-manship / Walter Zettl, with Paul Schopf and Jane Seigler.
       p. cm.
  Includes index.
   ISBN 978-0-939481-77-4
 1. Horses. 2. Horsemanship. 3. Horsemen and horsewomen. 4. Human-animal relationships. I. Schopf, Paul. II. Seigler, Jane. III. Title.
  SF285.Z48 2007
  636.1--dc22
                                    2007030699

table of contents

foreword

    I was very honored when asked by Herr Zettl to write the Foreword for his new book ***The Circle of Trust***. We are very fortunate to have such a truly knowledgeable horseman sharing his lifelong experience with us and combining the accumulated expertise of two continents in an easy-to-read volume.

    What this book makes absolutely clear is that when it comes to riding and particularly in dressage, it is the mutual respect of the two partners and their complete integration and attention to each other that leads to harmony and success. Herr Zettl's teaching stresses the soft, patient approach to reach the necessary ability without harm to the horse. There are no shortcuts when it comes to riding and his patient approach leads to enormous rewards.

    This is a book that is clear, simple and to the point and certainly very helpful to reach our goals if we are advanced or beginner dressage riders.

Dr. Max Gahwyler

acknowledgements

This book is dedicated to my good friends and long-time students Prof. Paul Schopf and his wife Jane Seigler, owners of Reddemeade Farm in Maryland. I cannot thank them enough for their help, without which this book would not be as it is today. Because of their knowledge of riding and of my philosophy, they know exactly what I am trying to say. In my mind it is really our book, a joint effort.

My hope is that this book may help all those who unite in a circle around our beautiful and most forgiving horses, who are dedicated to the equestrian sport and wish to assist us in making the horse's life easier.

Special thanks go to my wife Heide, who was very patient with me when I got up during the night, feeling compelled to write down my thoughts.

I also owe my gratitude to our girls Katja, Meike and their husbands Gordon and Derek for all their help with the English language and with the computer.

My friends in Munich, Drs. Christiane (who passed away after a long battle with cancer) and Hans Hebel, I thank for their understanding when, even on our vacations together, I worked on the book.

Special thanks also go to my publisher Elizabeth Carnes and her associate James Farber, who gave me the courage to get on with this second book; to Dr. Max Gahwyler who was so kind to write the foreword; to Harold Konink, who also helped me with my first book with his great knowledge of horses and to Bill Weber whose experience as a dressage rider as well as his linguistic talents enabled him to provide valuable editorial assistance.

Many thanks to Lynne Sprinsky and Cindy Sydnor who were always very helpful for any translations, and to Harry Zimmermann for his contribution about the Trakehner horses.

Last but not least I thank my friends Heidi Zorn and Mark Neihart who gave me the push to make the video tapes. They created those and were also a big help with this book.

Without my trainer, mentor and always my role model Colonel Herbert W. Aust, who taught me how to be a horseman and how to relate to both horses and people, it wouldn't have been possible to write this book. He deserves my endless thanks. He will be always in my heart.

If I forgot to mention anybody, I ask for forgiveness.

a horse's prayer

Give me to eat, give me to drink, and worry about me when the day's work is done, give me shelter, a clean bed and a wide box, talk to me, often your voice substitutes for the reins, be good to me and I will gladly serve you and love you. Don't jerk the reins, and forego the whip when we go up a rise. Don't hit or kick me should I not understand you, give me time to understand. Don't think me disobedient should I not follow your orders, perhaps the harness and hooves are not in order. Examine my teeth should I not eat, perhaps I have a bad tooth. You know how much that can hurt. Don't tie me too short and don't braid my tail, it is my only weapon against flies and mosquitoes. And at the end, dear master, when I am no longer useful, don't let me go hungry and cold and don't sell me. Don't give me to a new master, one who will torture me to death and let me starve, but give me a quick and compassionate death, dear master, and God will reward you, in this life and the next. Let me ask this of you, not in disrespect, when I request it in the name of Him who too was born in a stable, your savior Jesus Christ.

Amen

From an inscription in an old English barn

What I call the *Circle of Trust* is centered on the horse, which must always remain the focus and lodestar of our galaxy. Arrayed around him are the **breeder**, without whom we would not have horses; the **owner** and sponsor, financing and sustaining the horse; the **rider**, who signals to the horse through proper aids; the **trainer and/or instructor**, who guides the horse and rider into harmonic partnership; the **stable manager** and **groom**, who keep the horse happy, safe and secure; and the **judge**, who must recognize and reward correct training. Each has a critical influence on the welfare of our horses and the future of our sport.

Although much of what follows is couched in the language and context of the sport of dressage, the moral and ethical duties and responsibilities of all who touch our horses' lives cross all disciplines and interests.

Writing this book was for me the result of serious study of dressage and jumping, instilled through a life long dedication to professional horsemanship. The Circle of Trust is the essence of the important professional attitudes, responsibilities and approaches to a safe and productive long-term relationship with horses. The techniques and advice shared here come from generations of professionals working on improving their skills. Through the old Masters' experience we have everything from the shape and format of the dressage arena with the letters to the school figures and the Training Scale, all of which are aimed at producing horses who respond to our aids in a relaxed, light, but very powerful manner. But these teachings of the Masters are far from the exclusive purview of horse professionals. Indeed, the guidance given here is intended to help every horse breeder, owner, rider, teacher, judge, and farm owner. I have known amateurs who are more "professional" than professionals. They embrace "amateur" through its Latin root and pursue horsemanship for the love of the sport. On the other hand, I have seen amateurs (and unfortunately, "professionals") who give meaning to terms like "amateurish," who put themselves and their horses at serious risk through their lack of knowledge and concern.

Indeed, in my years of traveling and teaching all over Europe and North America, I have often been struck by the recklessness and/or ignorance of even those who have spent many years involved with horses. It is amazing that more serious accidents do not occur. The myths that horses are born knowing how to be ridden, that riding skills can be learned in a few weeks, that one "breaks" a horse, etc. are common parts of our literature and culture. Consider that horses are left in a pasture or small paddock for weeks without being exercised or even groomed, without enough food and water, and without being carefully inspected for illness or injury. Someone shows up once a month (or less), throws a saddle and bridle on, which many times don't fit the horse, and hacks off for many hours and days on this poor, unfit horse on a trail through rough terrain. It is a testament to the good nature of the horse and the benefits of luck that the outcome is an uneventful, pleasant walk. The rider is too afraid to do anything, the horse decides he likes the new scenery, and nothing untoward happens.

Consider also that busy, sometimes overworked stable managers can, over time, develop quite a blind eye to the myriad of hazards that can lurk in stalls, aisles, arenas, paddocks and pastures. This "blindness" is fostered by the fact that horses move around these hazards daily with no ill effects. Consider finally the rider, trainer and/or instructor who, faced with the pressure of a looming "important" competition and perhaps even with the permission of the owner, apply gadgets and "training methods" that force the horse to his physical and mental breaking point. More often than not the horse submits. It could show his pain by crying and screaming, but our loyal and always forgiving horse endures the torture inflicted by us quietly. But occasionally, things can (and do) go wrong. When they do, the results can be horrendous and dangerous.

It is my intention, with this book, to implore everyone involved with horses to acknowledge the mission and commitment of his or her chosen role—breeder, owner, trainer, instructor, rider, stable manager, groom, judge—and to steadfastly oppose the erosion of that mission and commitment in the face of fatigue or adversity. Only by doing so can we serve the highest and best interest of the horse, preserve his and our own well-being and safety, and thereby affirm our own humanity.

1

the horse

Adapt to the pace of Nature, Her secret is patience.

It is fitting and proper that the horse should be the center of our Circle. He is, after all, the reason you have opened this book. The horse is the most beautiful creature created by God, kind and forgiving. Emperors, kings and other influential personalities build monuments showing themselves on horseback to demonstrate their strength and power. But no monument could ever be sufficient to honor our kind horses, who give all their energy to please us. They forgive us our mistakes and ignorance, when we fail to understand their language and reactions.

In my earlier book ***Dressage in Harmony***, riding and training techniques are explored. But riding alone is not enough to ensure success. Everyone who comes in contact with a horse has an influence on him, at times just by providing a safe and quiet stable, at other times through specific training. This means that everyone who is included in the Circle should devote himself to understanding the nature and needs of the horse.

The horse is one of the strongest animals but very easily frightened. A little bird or a blowing scrap of paper, can cause him to leap into a panic. You can imagine how a horse must feel when a rider is on his back. With the rider's weight, legs, spurs, and whip, the horse senses the rider as a predator on his back. With his rough hands, the rider closes the door to the front where the horse could escape. The horse bucks and tries to run away, and for this he will be punished. Can you imagine how this poor, frightened animal must feel? We need lots of patience, understanding and love to make him our equal partner. It is our duty not to rob him of his personality and spirit while we seek to obtain his cooperation. "Domination" has no place in the training of horses.

In this endeavor, we must pursue two seemingly paradoxical goals. We seek to bring forth and foster his natural forward impulse while at the same time bringing him under control. We try to make him more brilliant and finer, so we can call on his compliance at any time without resistance. We hope to enable him to replicate his natural attitude found in the pasture—his free spirit, natural suspension and relaxation—while burdened with the task of carrying the rider.

At liberty, the horse is beautifully designed and perfectly in balance. But—from the first moment man climbed on his back—the rider presented the horse with a new problem, taking away his natural balance. The rider adds extra weight to the horse's forehand and becomes an additional, top-heavy appendage that is often laterally unstable. Over time, with correct training, the horse comes to understand and trust the weight of the rider. Even so, every day he must retrieve his balance with the weight of the saddle and the rider, no matter how far advanced the horse is in training. Ideally, this is obtained through the right rhythm, tempo and figures, adapted to the needs of each individual horse. More typically, it is sad to say, the rider bounces, tugs, pulls and kicks, and the horse learns that he can never trust just what the rider will do. His only safe strategy is to keep his body tense, and his feet close to the ground. This is no different from what we do when we have to perform a task that we know will be connected with pain. Naturally, we are tense and try to resist. With a back hollowed away from the rider's seat, the horse finds the lightest weight painful to carry. We round up our backs to make it easier to carry a heavy load, and we should show the horse how to do the same.

Freiherr v. Langen was the first German civilian show rider after World War I to be successful in international competition. He was famous for winning many shows with horses that many others would never take into training. When asked about his secret to his success with these "mediocre" horses, he would answer that it was no secret. "I love my horses and show them my love, and they love me and show me their love at home and in the show ring," he would say. Through correct handling and correct riding, one can make mediocre horses into stars, and through poor handling and riding super horses can be made average, or worse.

What is "Classical Training?" It is nothing else than being able to summon up what the horse shows in nature out of pleasure and high spirits. We attempt to achieve this without force, to make it more brilliant and bring it under our control, so that we can ask the horse to execute it anywhere and any time. Brilliance can only be borne of rhythm, tempo, relaxation, confidence, balance, and trust. The horse has to be trained precisely to the training scale, "rhythm-tempo, relaxation-contact, *Schwung*, straightness and collection," which leads to harmonious *Durchlässigkeit* (throughness). Even the "exercises above the ground," which, as Colonel Alois Podhajsky taught us, originate in the horse's natural play and self-expression, are simply a further step in the classical training.

Finally, we must understand that although our goal is to enhance the horse's natural beauty and brilliance, the horse in nature does not use himself in a way that makes it easy for him to carry a rider. The methods and techniques of classical training were developed to help the horse find a new balance and a new way of using his body, to make his task easier and more comfortable.

2 the breeder

Breeding matters. While talented trainers can bring out the best even in "ordinary" horses (and untalented trainers can destroy the potential of "super" horses), it is clear that selective breeding has led to more athletic, manageable, talented and enjoyable horses. The goal of a good breeding program is to produce horses that talented trainers can take beyond the current levels of excellence, and horses that are easier for serious amateurs to learn from, horses with conformation well suited to the task and superior attitude and character. In short, we would like every horse to be beautiful, athletic, kind, gentle, sound, healthy, calm. But some buyers look for "fire" and "brilliance," others for "safe and sound," some for black, some for paint. While there is great latitude for the goals of a breeding program, quality is always paramount, and care and commitment are the hallmarks of a good breeder.

Our first comment to breeders is a hearty "Thanks!" Without them we would have no sport, at least not to the level we have it now. Very few get rich through horse breeding, yet through their dedication and love of the horse they have carried us out of the darkness after World War II and our eternal gratitude is theirs.

2.1 Challenges to Modern Horse Breeding

Humans have managed the breeding of horses for over 5,000 years. Bedouins in Yemen (which is often referred to as the cradle of horse breeding) bred horses as early as between 3,200 and 3,000 BC, using a wild stallion named Hansabah and a mare called Baz. The stallion Zadel-Rakeb is said to be the original sire of the Arabian breed. Cave paintings depicting one of the first pedigrees of the world were dated back to this time. Successful breeding programs were so valued that a sultan who lived in the early 14th century paid 100,000 drachmas (about $1.5 million in today's currency) for an Arabian stallion. If we have been doing this for so long, haven't we figured it out yet?

Beautiful paddocks where horses can feel comfortable. This is Braeburn Farm, owned by Cindy and Dr. Sydnor.

It might come as a surprise, then, that in essence, modern sport horse breeding is only 50 years old: the shift of society away from the work horse to tractors, trucks and automobiles has had a huge impact on horse breeding. At the turn of the last century, horses were used so extensively for the army, transportation, and agriculture, that horse breeding was big business, led by strong guidance from the military and agricultural interests. Even up to World War II, horses were a large component of armies around the world. So many horses were lost in the war, and so reduced was the demand for horses immediately after the war, that a new effort had to be made to re-establish breeding programs. [1]

A heavy Clydesdale mare, owned by Penny Oneson-Dobas.

[1] See Appendix A for a history of the Trakehner breed.

On the one hand, the lessened demand for work horses meant that fewer breeders operated, and fewer people became expert horsemen. On the other hand, this change meant that breeding for sport horses became the main focus. The first breeding programs after the War were started by farmers, who bred the mares that remained to available stallions, to restablish their own herds.

Breeding for sport horses was slowly begun, producing a heavy warm-blood type from the working stock. Riders and trainers (largely in Europe) learned to work with these heavier warmbloods, like Fritz Thiedemann's Meteor, who became one of the most successful horses in the world through intensive training and gymnastic exercises. American riders, meanwhile, tried to develop dressage horses and jumpers from the ubiquitous Thoroughbred.

Fortunately, horse breeding has progressed far beyond the motto "cross a Thoroughbred with a Clydesdale" that was a popular amateur effort at one time. The European warmblood registries have made significant advances through strict testing and judicious out-crossing. Today, the resources available to a breeder are extensive and well indexed. The modern horse breeder must be well versed in the science of genetics, and must also have an extensive knowledge of the needs of dressage, jumping, eventing, driving and Western riding.

2.2 *Professional Breeding*

Professional breeding programs are highly dependent on careful selection, scientific research and long-term development. In Germany there are 15 *Landgestüte* or State owned breeding organizations, as well as private breeding facilities, that maintain the integrity of the various breeds. These organizations keep detailed records on every stallion and mare to provide a full bloodline on each approved breeding. Occasionally, a stallion will be brought in to the bloodline from another breed, but only after very careful consideration by the directors of the *Landgestüt*.

The Oldenburg stallion De Luxe, owned by Tina Beaman. Photo by Susan J. Stickle.

Mother and foal in an alert attitude.

Most breeding in Germany is done through these *Landgestüte*. They own most of the stallions. Young stallions are taken to a 70 day stallion test where they are evaluated. This involves a very stringent physical and mental training for the young stallions. Only the strongest and the best are approved for breeding. The *Landgestüte* might then buy the best stallion for inclusion in the State breeding program. Those who are not selected are typically gelded and sold as sport horses, with the exception of a few stallions that are used for sport. People wishing to breed their mares must be registered as breeders, and then apply to the organization for approval.

In Germany, the Federal Championship for horses and ponies is organized every year. Eligibility is limited to horses and ponies between three and six years of age, who have already shown successful results in each breed organization in dressage, jumping or driving competitions. These young horses must be very carefully prepared for this event, which requires a big effort, both mentally and physically. The champions in the different age groups are selected through a number of qualifying tests, leading to the final test. The horse with the highest percentage will be crowned champion.

Every breeder will try to turn one of his horses into champion. That is why he will breed his mares to the best stallions, and will also find the best rider to showcase the very best qualities of his horses at the championship and auctions. In this way the breeder can gain fame and command the highest price for his products.

In North America, the breeding of sport horses is much less structured and includes many small, amateur or "hobby" breeders.

Nevertheless, North American breeders are producing increasingly fine horses who can hold their own against their European counterparts.

2.3 Responsibilities

Owners of stallions and mares have a set of ethical responsibilities to their horses, their clients, and the sport. The stallion owner will have to go through the rigors of stallion testing, licensing and breed association approval. Stallion owners naturally assume that their horse is fine and suitable for breeding, but the owner's viewpoint is likely to be a bit biased. When the stallion testing goes poorly or the breed association fails to approve a stallion, it is best for the breed and the sport to accept the wisdom of the examiners who have lots of experience. Not every horse should become a breeding stallion, and this hard fact may be tough to accept at the moment, but it is necessary to ensure improvement of the breed.

Once the stallion is accepted, it is important for the owner to accept only appropriate mares. The foal is the product of both the mare and stallion, and over the long term, it will be the quality of the foals that determines the stallion's reputation. Recognizing the shortcomings of the stallion, and devising a breeding strategy to overcome them may take a little time. If you cross a vicious but highly trainable dog with a gentle, un-trainable one, you may hope for a gentle, trainable puppy, but end up with a vicious, untrainable one. Similarly with horses, the mix of traits may not come out as you expect. Some pairings will work well, so the stallion owner needs to know the history of his stallion's line and the general outcome of crossing with other breed lines.

The mare owner needs to take similar care, and has the same responsibility to the sport—breeding only mares with good health, no hereditary unsoundness, and good conformation and disposition. The mare owner has the added long-term responsibility to provide excellent health care for mare and foal.

2.4 Amateur Breeding

It is most important for an amateur breeder to work with good horses. Breeding a low quality mare with conformation problems or poor temperament is irresponsible. Perhaps the most common form of amateur breeding is the breeding of a performance mare who has perhaps reached an age where competition is no longer of paramount importance, or who has suffered a sidelining injury. Having a foal from a quality mare can be a rewarding and enjoyable endeavor. The project carries with it, how-

The Trakehner stallion Donaufürst, owned by Erin Brinkman. Photo by Dean Graham.

Insightful, a Trakehner brood mare, owned and bred by Jean Brinkman, Gestüt Valhalla. Photo also by Jean Brinkman.

ever, all the responsibility for the safety, health and handling of the foal that is assumed by the professional breeder.

The first problem is to find a suitable stallion. Find an experienced professional who can give advice and help make the proper selection. While a stallion can cover many mares in a season, the mare owner will have only a few chances to make the "right" match. This is really why breeding records focus on the stallions and not the mares—genetics is a science of statistics, and the statistics can tell a lot for a stallion who has a hundred offspring. It can not tell much about the mare who has one or two foals in her life. As a mare owner, therefore, making the right choice is very difficult. Unfortunately, the most expert people in horse breeding usually run a breeding operation of their own that is often based on a few stallions. It should come as no surprise, therefore, that such an expert will decide that one of his stallions is "just perfect" for your mare. Talk to several experts at several breeding farms. Learn as much as you can. In the end, you will want to know why you have chosen the stallion you did, and you will need to be comfortable with your choice.

What not to do

Don't assume that horses can mate by themselves because they evolved in herds in the wild. Those horses were always on the move and were tough adapters in a big, open land. Even so, many mothers and foals died. The success of the breed does not depend on every mare and foal surviving, but the success of your mare and foal does.

The next problem is to decide upon foaling arrangements. Breeding goes far beyond selecting stallion and mare, supervising insemination, and hoping everything comes out OK. Breeding is a commitment to the next generation. It is about foals. The Olympic champion starts as a foal, just like every other horse. The successful breeding operation must look beyond the polished brass in the stallion's barn and the promotional videos. Attention must be paid to the foaling stall, facilities for 24-hour foaling watch, ready access to veterinary care, and knowledgeable, professional staff to assist at delivery. The staff should be trained to recognize any abnormalities, and have a well thought out and well rehearsed plan for what to do at every stage. The simplest solution for the amateur is to find a local breeding farm that is well set-up for foaling, with professional staff and equipment for foal watch. You will need to rely on their professionalism and expertise, so be sure you are comfortable with their abilities and facilities.

If you are going to arrange for home delivery, you should create an environment as close to a professional operation as you can. Be prepared to wait longer than the thirty minutes you expect for your pizza delivery man to show up. Foal watch can be a long and tiring process. You will need lots of reliable friends or staff, and you need to be available on a moment's notice. Work with your vet from very early on, getting enough information and equipment and supplies to be able to handle emergencies alone.

Once the foal is born, you need to provide for safe accommodation for the mare and foal. If you can, find a friend or other horseman in the area who will also have at least one other mare and foal so that you can build a small "herd." Either arrange to take your mare to your friend's, or offer to take theirs. Decide based on the facilities available, safety, and experience.

Up to the time of weaning foals and mares should be kept in groups, so the youngsters can develop friendships and play, to build character and establish herd social skills. The pastures must be extremely safe. Things that would never interest an older horse can easily become intriguing to a foal: they can try to eat poisonous plants, get into tight places, and generally find trouble in any way they can. They run clumsily, often out-running their ability to stop and turn, and frequent collisions with fences, trees, whatever, can lead to injury. Foals seem more susceptible to illness than a pre-school child! Proper vaccinations and constant watching of their health is a fundamental requirement.

2.5 Breeders: The Foal's First Trainers

As the saying goes, "You only get one chance to make a good impression." In my discussion of the trainer, I will focus on building confidence and trust between the horse and rider under saddle. But the real start of this training happens with the fair and proper handling of the foal. The early acceptance of human guidance will have a big influence on the mature horse's attitude toward work. The earlier the handling of the foal starts, the easier it is to keep the situation under control. As early as possible they should learn to have their feet lifted up and checked, getting ready for handling by farriers and grooms. Leading a young foal alongside a mare on the way to and from the pasture can be an exciting task, but very important. Experience and patience are extremely valuable here. You need to keep control without resorting to violence, so the young horse learns respect and not fear, that he learns that we are friends. (Hopefully, he won't think we are playmates.)

Weaning is one of the most traumatic times of the horse's life. It is best to start in the stall, separating the mare and foal with a partition through which they can still see and snuffle each other. Depending on how this goes, you can then try mare and foal in adjoining stalls, where they can still have some small contact. When it comes time to separate mares and foals permanently, it is best to do this in groups. The foals are in their familiar pasture while the mares are removed, preferably to a close-by pasture, so they still have a distant contact.

Young horses need to grow up in herds, in space where they can play and develop muscles, lungs, social skills and a happy outlook for life. We have seen young foals kept by themselves, soon after weaning, who have no friends to play with, or herds of foals kept in such small spaces that they cannot run and frolic. Both situations are essentially abusive and lead to developmental problems like depression and fighting, and bad character.

As the weanlings develop, play and socialization are key to their physical and emotional development. While it is not good to start young horses into work too early, which causes physical and mental troubles that will stay with the horse throughout his career, it is also not good to turn them out without any human contact. Keep human interaction through at least daily handling, grooming and check-ups.

2.6 *Passing Along the Circle of Trust*

The breeder has started our process. By rigorous study, careful selection, diligence in breeding and foaling, proper veterinary care, well-managed pastures and safe surroundings, the breeder has seen to it that our horse has arrived in this world, ready to start the long journey to becoming a champion. The breeder has a financial interest in his business - getting a fair price, covering expenses, making a profit. But the breeder also has an emotional, ethical and financial interest in seeing that the foal remains at the center of our Circle of Trust—with owners, trainers and riders able and committed to taking him to the heights. The renown that follows the breed show champion and performance horse champion flows back to the credit and reputation of the breeder. It is a very short-sighted breeder who takes the sales profit and ignores the future that lies in store for his foals. The successful breeder is very closely connected to the quality and skill of the owner, trainer and riders. All are connected in our Circle of Trust.

Foal and breeder in full confidence and trust. Breeder Robin Littlefield's farm is My Tara Mist. Photo by Gail Brooks.

3
the owner

I separate the owner from the trainer and rider in our Circle, although as many will attest, they are often one and the same individual. We are familiar with the separate roles in horse racing—the wealthy owner, paying the bills; the professional trainer, managing the horse; and the jockey, riding the race. At the top of other equestrian sports, we also find wealthy owner-sponsors, professional trainers and top level, essentially professional riders. But whether the owner is a separate person or is also the rider (and perhaps trainer), the role of owner is our subject here. So if you own and ride your horse, take some time as rider to give yourself thanks and appreciation for the support and contribution that you make as owner.

The owners make the sport possible. They pay the bills and enable the entire industry to exist: breeders, riders, trainers, vets, farriers, judges and all of the various businesses that surround the sport horse industry. They get the pride and satisfaction of having chosen a promising horse, seeing him through training in the hands of a capable trainer, and entrusting him to a gifted rider to achieve great things. None of the choices along this way are particularly easy, and disaster in the form of injury or disease can abruptly stop even the best laid plans, yet the dedicated owner understands the difficulty and pitfalls and continues on, seeking the great reward that comes from putting everything together into a successful sporting career.

The owner is ultimately responsible for the well being of the horse. His duty is to choose wisely and to supervise the care, training and riding for the benefit, health and safety of the horse. Abusive training, unsafe stabling, or poor riding cannot be hidden away and/or tolerated by the conscientious owner. As the "chairman of the board," the owner is responsible for the hiring (and firing) of the operating officers (trainers, stable managers, rider).

3.1 Choose Wisely: Buying a Horse

The first step for an owner is becoming an owner—that is, purchasing or otherwise acquiring a horse. Of all the issues that face the future owner, the most daunting can be the initial purchase: getting just the right horse for you. Some people rush out and buy a horse without thinking; some try so hard to find the perfect horse that they never actually buy one. The best policy is somewhere between these extremes. Buy carefully, but not obsessively. The careful buyer considers why she wants to own a horse, then determines the age, training level, general conformation and temperament that are needed to satisfy her desires. Next, she looks at her budget and time availability and starts a search. Many of the training and management difficulties that arise with a horse can be avoided by selecting the right horse in the first place. On the other hand, the obsessive buyer thinks that all training and management difficulties can be avoided if she just picks the right horse in the first place. There will be plenty of time later to make mistakes in the management and training, and just as no horse is perfect when purchased, no horse remains perfect, healthy and sound through their life.

So what does "choosing wisely" mean? There are eight steps to choosing wisely:
1. Decide why you want to own a horse.
2. Determine what qualities you need to satisfy that desire.
3. Be realistic.
4. Decide on a budget.
5. Get professional help.
6. Search and learn the market.
7. Understand the vetting process.
8. Consider the future.

Why do you want to own a horse?

Do you want a pet—an animal that you are going to care for? Do you have aspirations to be an equestrian competitor and need a partner? Are you looking for a means of transportation to explore the countryside? Are you looking for a status symbol? Are you trying to fulfill a childhood romantic fantasy?

These questions are routinely dismissed by prospective owners, because they seem to be an inconvenient stumbling block in their rush to fulfill their desire. And then they end up with the wrong horse. It is fundamentally the moral and ethical responsibility of the owner to be brutally honest with yourself about why you want to buy a horse, and then to think of whether you are equipped and have the resources to execute that plan. For example, if you decide that you want to buy a horse because you want to be a successful competitor at the national level, you may decide to buy a fancy, big moving young horse. But if you are an amateur rider with a full time job and a family, so you can only ride two or three times per week, and have only average talent, you are unlikely to have success with that horse. He would require daily riding by a trainer with an advanced and experienced seat and knowledge. It is a squandering of your and your horse's time to go for this horse. Perhaps that horse could be bought by an amateur whose goal is to have (and pay for) a professional rider and trainer. But our working, family-oriented amateur might better buy an experienced schoolmaster horse without such lofty gaits on whom the owner/rider can easily learn and have fun.

Are you a rider, or are you an owner? If you answer this question with "I want to own a horse so I can ride," then you should seriously question whether you need to become an owner or whether you should explore the many other ways that you can ride a horse owned by someone else—lesson barns, riding clubs, leasing, etc. There are many owners who have overestimated their ability to get out and ride their horse or who have taken on a second horse or have semi-retired horses that need exercise and care. Any of these options can fill your needs if you are a "rider," not an "owner" at heart, or if your circumstances do not permit you to take on the responsibility of ownership.

Assessing the qualities you need

Once you are clear on why you want a horse, you need to consider the qualities that you need. Some issues to consider are: age, training, conformation, quality of gaits, temperament and health.

Age. If you are looking for a schoolmaster, you should not be looking at a horse less than 8 years old. Generally, they will be 15 or older—often a healthy 20-year-old will give the highest level of training for an affordable price. If you are looking for a competition horse to grow with, you should not be looking at 18-year-olds. But only very experienced trainers should be looking at young horses. Young horses are so fragile and impressionable, and can so easily be set on the wrong path, that their training and riding should be left to trainers who are particularly qualified to work with youngsters. Of course there are no hard and fast rules here, but the key thing is to consider where you want to be today, where you want to be in a few years, and finally what plans you can make for the horse's retirement.

Training Level. The work that goes into training a horse up the levels shows up clearly in the price. The level of training should be considered together with the horse's age: a 6-year-old that is at First Level dressage is quite different from the 15-year-old also at First Level. It is quite normal for the 6-year-old to be at this level in the hands of a good trainer, and has much further to go. The 15-year-old has probably had intermittent or poor training, and has likely developed his own comfort level for this work. Such a horse would be a good candidate for an amateur without aspirations for the show ring, but a poor choice for those with serious competition plans.

Conformation. Good conformation makes it much easier for a horse to do the work required. In short, that is a definition of good conformation. Easier is better. There is no benefit to working against conformation flaws. If you have to accept a horse with a conformation problem, you will always face the issue throughout the training. On the other hand, there is no horse with perfect conformation, so the wise buyer is educated about conformation strengths and weaknesses and what they will mean for the training.

Quality of Gaits. Along with conformation, you should consider the basic quality of the horse's gaits. The older the horse, the more likely it is that the gaits that you see are the gaits you will have. But I would really like to emphasize that bigger is not always better—a beginning rider looking for a schoolmaster, or an ambitious amateur with competitive aspirations may end up with a horse with huge gaits that are simply too difficult to sit. A good rule is to never buy a horse whose trot you cannot sit on the day you try it.

Temperament. Good temperament makes it much easier to train and work with a horse. In short, that is a definition of good temperament. Easier is still better. There are two aspects to temperament—ground manners and ridability. The two are not always related. Some horses can be difficult to handle in the stall, but very agreeable to work under the saddle, and vice versa. Horses that are difficult when being ridden are actually revealing basic mistakes in the training, and can be quite dangerous. These are not for inexperienced riders, and those looking for a show horse are best counseled to look elsewhere, because even though you might get a "bargain" for the difficult horse, you pay for it over and over when you don't "train" so much as you "deal with" the problems.

Health. Everyone wants a perfectly healthy horse, with no "scratches or dents." When buying a horse, you should seek the advice of a well-qualified veterinarian who can assess general health and soundness and report to you on his findings. The older the horse, the more likely that small problems will arise in the joints, eyes, heart, etc. I have known of excellent schoolmasters who had significant joint problems or heart valve problems, who gave years and years of service to riders who made their first shows at Prix St. Georges and Intermediaire on them, supported by careful therapeutic and veterinary treatment. These riders could not have afforded sound, younger horses at these levels, but could afford to take the risk associated with these problems. I have also seen such horses fail before too long, so you have to be very aware of the risk, and accept it as the price of "tuition" for the excellent education these fine, old "equine professors" can provide.

Be realistic

One seller once told me "I'm not selling horses, I'm selling dreams." For many, many buyers, this is indeed true. The buyer imagines what great things will come from that pretty young colt, or that "with good training, we can correct that tendency to go downhill and he will go like a champion." If you have never taken a horse from that shuffling gait to the pinnacle of lofty strides, then you are asking for disappointment. The best advice is to "buy the horse you see that day." Try and close your eyes to what might be, and assess what is there right now. If you are looking for a horse to show at second level, are the walk-canter transitions clear and balanced? Is the shoulder-in easy and steady? Today. Are they repeatable —that is, of the five or so walk-canter transitions that you see or ride, is only one good, or is only one bad? The less experienced the rider, the more there seems to be a tendency to imagine, and the more that this is a problem. If you are experienced and looking for a young prospect to start, you may be thinking ahead, but you still have to be careful to evaluate what is there today. In this case the basic gaits, conformation, temperament and health are the important factors, so be sure they are good right now.

Decide on your budget

The challenge here is to find the best horse for your purposes within the budget that you have available. Since the price of one horse can be 1000 times greater than another, it seems that there is always a budget issue. A corollary to that principle is that the same horse may be offered at very different prices, depending on where and by whom it is being sold. I cannot tell someone what his budget limit should be, nor give advice on how much over budget he should go to get a better horse. What I can advise is that you should start by determining what you want to spend, and then carefully look for the horses with the best qualities to meet your needs and desires in that price range.

It will be important to remember what you are looking for—don't go shopping for a schoolmaster and come home with a two-year-old colt! You can change your mind about what you want, but remember all the research and shopping you have done for the schoolmaster. Now you need to do the same for two-year-olds. Just because the seller with a (lame) schoolmaster tries to talk you in to his other "super" young horse in the next stall is no reason to jump! Many times we have heard of people shopping for schoolmasters who end up with overly hot competition horses or raw youngsters with much more spirit than they can ever handle.

Get professional help

Usually when we buy a horse, we are looking for something "better" than we had before: more talented, higher trained, or a super talented, new young prospect. The buyer is usually entering slightly new territory. This is obviously true for the first-time buyer, but it is also true at the higher levels. Get help from someone with more experience than yourself. A trusted partner can guide you and help you see pros and cons that you may otherwise miss.

Learn the market

How much should you pay? What is the "fair value"? How do you know? In truth, the way to know the value is to know the market. If you know that there are five other similar horses priced lower than the one you are looking at, then you need to ask what is special about this one? Dealers and professionals who buy and sell many horses know the market fairly well, and can quickly snatch up a bargain, but the amateur has trouble knowing whether the price is good or not. If you are taking the time to find a talented horse of the proper age, with good conformation and soundness, then take the time to study the market as well. Read the ads and compare the prices and qualities of the horses to the ones that you look at.

Understand the vetting process

With reasonable research and education, you can evaluate conformation, age, temperament and ride-ability. When it comes to soundness and health, you need to get a professional veterinary examination. The vet will examine the horse for general health and clinical soundness, and can perform further diagnostic tests on joints, respiratory capacity, drug screens, etc. Depending on the price, age and intended use of the horse, you may choose to have a more or less exhaustive examination. Consult with the veterinarian to understand what is appropriate. You should also know that the vet will not give a "buy" or "no buy" recommendation. She will tell you what she finds, what findings are of concern, what she sees as good. You then need to go back to your original plan for buying a horse and decide for yourself whether the vet's opinion is consistent with what you want, or not.

The unwanted horse

A major problem that is coming more and more into the public consciousness is that of the "unwanted horse." When you become the owner of a horse, you have a responsibility to consider what you will do when he becomes old or injured, or your own abilities outgrow his. Do you have the facilities and resources to care for the horse through retirement? If you plan to keep him for only a few years, you may believe that you will be able to sell the horse and that some other person will assume the responsibility for care. But what do you plan to do if the horse becomes injured, and you are unable to sell? A horse is not a piece of sporting equipment that can be used for a few months, then stowed in the back of the closet for lack of interest. In fact, it is to be expected that as the horse becomes older, he will require more care and expense, even when his showing days are over. Over the years, you will have taken a lot of enjoyment from your horse. This you should pay back with love, care and respect, to ensure a good retirement for your long-time friend.

3.2 Supervising the Care

Stabling

Now that you have become an owner, you have the responsibility to care for your horse—to provide shelter, food, water and exercise. In their natural habitat, horses evolved as animals who roamed wide territories, grazing constantly. Except when threatened by predators, they moved primarily at the walk. Therefore their life generally did not include periods of intense eating, intense exercise, and extended confinement in a small space. Obviously, the realities of life for the modern sport horse have come to include all of these. So our goal in managing our horse must be to, as much as possible, make his life conform to his nature, and where not possible, to reduce the stress created by the unnatural requirements we impose on him.

Some owners care for their horses themselves at home. Others entrust the care to a hired stable manager. Still others send their horses to a boarding facility. In all cases, however, the ultimate responsibility for horse's health, safety and well being remains squarely on the shoulders of the owner. The guiding principle is this: take extra steps to reduce the stress felt by the horse.

He should feel comfortable and safe in his surroundings. Everyone working around horses needs to be calm, quiet and have great patience. The horse's stall is his home. His time in his stall is a time for peace and rest. It is important that we respect

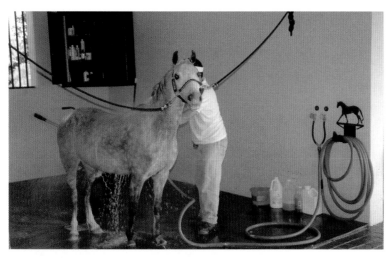

Two SwanS Farm. Owner, Carol Cohen. Groom, John. Photo by Mark Neihart.

this and provide an environment that is well ventilated, clean, quiet and safe. As herd animals, communication with other horses is important. They should be able to see and hear other horses, but not be permitted to fight or harass each other over the stall partitions. Move horses that don't get along with their neighbors.

Ideally, the stall gives the horse quiet time without a lot of activity up and down the aisles. The aisles should be wide enough so that other horses being walked by will not excite those already in their stalls and incite them to bite the passing horse.

My old master rolled out a rug in every aisle after mucking out, so every step of the horse was silent. Nowadays rubber bricks or mats are popular for this purpose.

Hacking is most important for the horse's body and soul. Linda Hoover on her horse Finnegan. Photo by Ken Westcott.

A wide barn aisle, with rubber footing to avoid slipping. This is Candlewood Farm, owned by Neil Schwartzberg. Photo by Jane Casnellie.

But the best stabling for the horse is no substitute for time in pasture and exercise. Every week the horse's regular work should include jumping under the rider, hacking through fields and trails, or extended time in a pasture. There are some instances when turn-out is problematic— such as for stallions who fight with other horses, or horses who race around, injuring themselves and exciting other horses, or in some cities and suburbs where there is insufficient space. Some horses even seem to dislike extended turn-out, and after a short time will begin to pace or wait by the gate. One would do better to let those horses out by themselves, or give them more exercise, including perhaps working them more than once a day as a way to get full relaxation. Only when the horse is completely relaxed in the training can we ask him for the most difficult work without overstressing him.

Relaxation also keeps the horse from developing bad habits in the stable. The more limited the turn out, the more important it is that the horse be brought to complete relaxation in training, in order for him to regain the natural balance that is eroded by the restricted movement that extended stall confinement implies. Just as bad training leads to a horse that does not look forward to entering the arena, rough handling in the barn, poor stabling and too much noise and activity will lead a horse to stress, unhappiness, nervousness and fearfulness in the barn. The poor horse that gets both improper training and bad treatment in the barn will have nothing to look forward to. The once quiet and willing horse becomes frightened, shies from almost everything and gets more and more tense. A once promising horse ends up sour or a nervous wreck. When turned out, these horses will often be hard to catch. They can even come to dislike being turned out, spending this otherwise precious time trying to hide—or becoming dangerous fighters. It is the owner's job to ensure that the horse's environment reduces or eliminates these stressors as much as possible.

Safety

Taking proper care also means paying attention to safety. And safety means prevention. It is ultimately the owner's responsibility to ensure that whoever performs the role of stable manager (himself or someone else) keeps his eyes constantly open for potential problems and hazards.

Fire is the most dangerous hazard in the barn. First and foremost, good fire prevention is essential. Smoking, faulty electrical wiring, tangled extension cords and overloaded circuits are threats to your horse's life. Dust and spider webs are a constant problem in barns, and can collect within electrical boxes, fan motors, switches and lighting fixtures. Space and bucket heaters that are left on after use, as well as fans that are not checked and cleaned regularly, could all very easily lead to a terrible fire.

Fire extinguishes need to be properly located and easy to reach, of the proper type and size, and regularly checked for charging. Everybody working in the stable should be familiar with their proper operation, without first having to read the instructions. Easily inflammable materials like gasoline and oil, hay and shavings, and equipment like motorcycles, tractors, lawn mowers and cars should not be stored close to each other or to the barn. Electrical cables need to be protected so that rodents (or nosy horses) cannot reach and chew on them.

Farm management should consult with the local fire department to know exactly where the nearest fire hydrant is and, if none, how and where water can be obtained. In some areas, the fire department will come to facilities to familiarize themselves with access to the barns, the availability of water, the electrical configuration, and so on. It is wise to arrange for such visits so that there is less confusion in the event of an emergency.

A well manicured, bright and airy stall, with shavings banked higher alongside the walls. This is also Candlewood Farm. Photo by Jane Casnellie.

These recommendations may sound like the way a modern, large commercial facility should be expected to operate. And indeed, such facilities generally have the luxury of adequate income and resources to hire professional consultants, build new barns with particular care for fire safety, fire equipment access, and so on. But such facilities are by far in the minority. Many horsemen operate out of old facilities, perhaps charming bank barns, old cow barns, etc. Bills for feed, hay, labor, fence and pasture maintenance, equipment repair, insurance, and on and on compete with the needs for fire safety measures. But there is something wrong with the picture of a new tractor or shining horse trailer parked outside of a charming old barn that needs a new electrical system. The horror of a barn fire is something I would never wish on anyone. For a personal farm, the loss is devastating emotionally. For a small commercial barn, a fire can be a killing blow to the business. Even if the horses can be saved, customers will leave and new ones slow to come.

It should also be emphasized that renovating an old barn is not a license to relax. We have heard horror stories of barn fires caused by new wiring. Regardless of the competence and professional standards of licensed electricians, mistakes can occur, and it is wise to pay particular vigilance to the barn safety immediately after any electrical work. The price of safety is eternal vigilance!

Unfortunately, the best prevention measures can only reduce the risk of fire, they can not eliminate it. In the event of a fire, the second line of defense is a well-prepared and well rehearsed action plan, familiar to all employees and shared with appropriate customers such as boarders and working students. The first job is to get people and horses out of danger. Every horse should have a halter and lead shank kept by the stall door, or better yet, the horses could wear a halter at all times, so that they can be led to safety without delay.

Horses that have been evacuated from the barn should be put in a safe, fenced-in pasture or paddock, not just chased out of the barn. A terrified horse will often seek out his place of safety and refuge—his stall—and simply run back into the burning barn, where he expects to find safety and security. If horses are usually turned out in herds or small groups, it may be better to turn them all out quickly into one convenient pasture than to waste time figuring out where everyone goes.

Care

The next responsibility of the owner is to ensure that the horse receives excellent regular care as well as any emergency treatments that might be needed. The key members of this team are the veterinarian, farrier, stable manager and groom.

Veterinarian. Veterinary medicine is a science, subject to the same rapid advances as human medicine, and a wise owner will retain a qualified veterinarian as soon as she brings a new horse home. Work with the vet to establish a regular schedule for inoculations, worming and check-ups. If you are boarding your horse with someone else, find out whom they consult for veterinary service and satisfy yourself that the management and vet work together for the interest of your horse. Regardless of whether you board your horse or keep him in your own stable, get to know the vet and let him know of your commitment to your horse, e.g., whether you would author-ize surgery if needed. An emergency is not the best time to start a relationship with your vet.

Farrier. Farriers are skilled professionals and their work is critical to your horse's long term health and soundness. Dealing with a blacksmith requires the same level of trust, respect and communication as you have with your vet. You should be able to talk with him about the shoeing of your horse, and you should respect his judg-ment and expertise. Make sure the farrier can also work well with your vet, if and when corrective or therapeutic shoeing becomes necessary.

Consult the farrier in making decisions about whether and when shoeing is nec-essary. In my time we let the young horses go as long as possible without shoes. The same was true for horses in full training. We took the shoes off as soon as the show season was over, so the hoof could grow, and the elasticity of the hoof was not influ-enced by the shoes.

Nutrition. The nutritional and digestive needs of the horse are the elements that are probably the most deeply compromised by the stabling and confinement we impose on these essentially nomadic, grazing animals. The late *Reitmeister* Herr von Neindorff, at his *Reitinstitut* in Karlsruhe, personally supervised the feeding of his horses five times per day, because in nature the horse eats small quantities constant-ly—a full stomach might interfere with his ability to flee. Horses in work may be sup-plemented with grain, but constant access to hay is always required to replicate the horse's grazing nature. Equally important, of course, is a continual supply of water and access to salt.

In the past, prescriptions for feeding horses were fairly basic. With the growth of the sport horse industry, feed companies and vet schools have taken on much more research into the nutritional needs of the athletic sport horse. Consensus is changing on the proper balance of protein, fat, carbohydrates, and the role of processed feed in supplementing the various kinds of hay now available. Owners must keep themselves educated as nutritional science develops.

Dentist. Here again, our management of the horse in an unnatural way, with stall confinement and processed grain for feed, creates problems that must be addressed. In the wild, rough, low quality forage kept the horse's teeth (which grow continually throughout his life) in proper shape for efficient eating. When a stabled horse lacks interest in eating, has problems with the bit or drops his food, it may be that his teeth are hurting because they have grown irregular or they are too sharp. A check-up by the dentist every 6 months should be sufficient to keep problems from arising.

Emergencies. The owner has the ultimate responsibility for the care of his horse. If the horse is boarded at a stable, the stable management may be much more experienced than the owner in dealing with trouble. However, even though manage-ment should advise the owner on what to do, the responsibility for all the important decisions still rests with the owner.

By definition, emergencies are unexpected, and require a quick response. When they occur it is too late to start coming up with a plan. From the moment you become a horse owner, you need to have a clear idea of how emergencies will be handled. Of course, you cannot foresee every situation, but you should have a general plan as well as specific plans for colic, acute lameness, etc.

The important elements of a plan are:

1. Know how to recognize an emergency.
2. Know basic first aid.
3. Establish a contact list.
4. Have a backup plan.
5. Know where to go.

First and foremost, an emergency situation needs to be detected—the daily caregiver needs to know the signs of colic, choking and other health abnormalities. They need to keep a close eye on horses that come in from pasture to identify any cuts or bruises. In virtually all cases, early detection is a most important part of successful treatment.

Next, the owner and veterinarian are contacted, as necessary. If the situation is acute, the caregiver should contact the veterinarian immediately, even if he cannot reach the owner. The caregiver needs to have a current list of all the telephone numbers of the owner, and know the best way to reach him at any time. In case the owner cannot be reached, the caregiver should have advance authorization to decide what needs to be done in case of colic, acute lameness, injury, and so on. For boarded horses, such authorization is best included in the boarding contract. If there is insurance coverage on the horse, the caregiver should know how to contact the insurance company and have any policy numbers that might be required.

Emergencies seem to happen at the worst times. You should have a plan for what to do if your emergency occurs after hours—does your vet practice keep a 24-hour on-call service? Is your regular vet located an hour away but another lives close by? Or do you have to stock sufficient medications and become skilled in their use so that you can work with your vet over the phone? Not everyone has 10 board-certified equine vets within a 20-minute drive of the barn.

If there is an equine veterinary hospital within reach, be sure that you know where the facility is, and exactly how you are going to get your horse there. Do you have your own truck and trailer? Does your barn have one? Is it kept fueled, hooked up and ready? Can you be sure of using it at any time, or would you need to reach the barn owner? Is it away at shows often? What is your backup plan?

Finally, the owner should decide ahead of time the level of treatment he is willing or able to pursue. A horse in his prime without other major health concerns will likely be a candidate for emergency medical treatment. The difficult situations are those where the horse is old or has a history of other medical problems. The simple choice of "spare no expense, do whatever is necessary" is no longer so simple.

The difficult choice between treatment or euthanasia is the owner's. This decision is the last, great responsibility of horse ownership, and hopefully can be made with the assistance of a knowledgeable, understanding veterinarian. Sometimes this decision necessarily will be driven by the anticipated expense of treatment. The existence of adequate medical and surgical insurance can make the decision easier, but other issues such as quality of life during and after recovery can also factor in. This is never an easy decision, but it should be made in a way that will leave the owner with a clear conscience, if a heavy heart.

3.3 Choosing Trainers and Riders

As the horse owner, you are the chairman of the board and CEO. You are responsible for hiring the Chief Operating Officer (the trainer) and senior staff (the rider). As with any good business, you need to hire the best people you can for these positions, then let them do their work. You need to keep an eye on what is happening, but not interfere with day-to-day operations. In this section we will discuss how to find a good trainer that you can trust, how to monitor the activity without interfering and what to do when you feel a different direction is needed.

How to find someone good

There one basic reason for hiring a trainer: because you want someone who is more experienced than you to lead the development of the horse. If it is because you simply don't have the time to dedicate to training your own horse, then you should still try and find someone more experienced than you to lead the training. If you try to give the job to someone you cannot trust, or whose skills you do not believe to be superior to your own, then you will find yourself always meddling in their work, correcting and criticizing them. So you have to set about finding someone you respect, someone with more experience, and someone you can work with. This applies whether you have an Olympic hopeful that you are sending across the country to work with a top trainer, or want to keep your horse locally and ride it yourself.

Where to start? The first place to look is at the show grounds. Find out who is training the horses that you like. Watch the warm-up ring as well as the show ring. Look into the stabling areas and see how professionally the whole operation is run. Be aware that despite the stress of the show, people usually try to be on their best behavior at such public venues. If you see trainers losing their patience with horses or riders, you can assume that they are not very patient at home, either. On the other hand, some trainers' clients can try the patience of any saint, so watch the overall conduct of the trainer as well. If there are lots of riders, you can get a better sense of the trainer's method. If the trainer has just a few riders at the show, you might have to watch the schedule closely to catch the warm-ups and rides. In the end, you should come away with some ideas of who you might like and who you will stay away from.

You can get more ideas by asking friends, other owners and riders, other trainers and judges you might know. Consult local dressage or eventing organizations. You can get some good advice, and learn lots of gossip, from the local horse community. Be aware that gossip is gossip, and subject to lots of distortion. Treat this information as suspect but potentially useful. For instance, if a prominent trainer is rumored to be moving to your area, you might hear it first via the gossip mill, but if it turns out to be true, you will of course want to know.

Now that you have a list of possible candidates, go watch lessons being taught and horses being trained. Contact the trainer, tell him of your interest and ask for permission to come and watch. If he is rude, hesitant or reluctant, cross him off your list. When you visit the facility, look at the organization, the cleanliness and care taken with the horses, the safety of the grounds, the decorum and competence of everyone around. People who know what they are doing surround themselves with others who approach their own tasks professionally.

Watch the training sessions. Don't intrude, but quietly observe the handling and preparation of the horses. Pay attention to the warm-up, and keep your eyes open to other riders on the premises. If the trainer has a "system", it should be reflected not only in his own work, but in the work of his students. Except in the case where a facility has many trainers, the philosophy and attitude of the trainer will show itself throughout the operation, even in riders not working directly with the trainer.

Watch carefully the work with "difficult" horses. Why is the horse difficult? Is it in fact the trainer's own method that creates the problem? Are the horses over-worked? Are they under-worked? Are only the "stars" given the trainer's full attention? Imagine your horse at this barn. What kind of work and handling will he receive? If you have called for an appointment to come and watch, you can be sure that any problem will be thoroughly explained to you, such as "we just got this horse in for training, and his owner really messed him up," or "He is recovering from a stone bruise, he will be OK in a week or so." Sometimes these statements are true, often they are slight exaggerations crafted to protect the trainer's reputation: "just got this horse" may mean they had it for a year, and have not been able to do anything with it.

If things seem to go well, and you are satisfied with the trainer's method, take some time to talk with him and get a sense of his character. It will be important that you can talk freely and comfortably and develop a relationship that you feel will work toward the benefit of all—you, the trainer, and most important, the horse.

Deferring to someone else's judgment

Now that you have found your trainer, you need to establish your working relationship. Remember that you have engaged the trainer to be responsible for the development of your horse. You have selected someone with more experience and knowledge of horses, so you should defer to his judgment in the daily work. It is just as you would do in choosing a school for your child: you examine the quality of care and the environment, and match the nature of the school to the personality of the child. But once you have chosen the school, you must let the well-trained and experienced faculty do the teaching. If you find out later that you don't approve of something, you don't step in to tell the teacher how to teach. You either come to accept the problem or change schools, depending on the size of your concern. So it should be working with a trainer. The owner should, of course, be free to come anytime to see his horse and the training. It is reasonable for him to show interest in his horse, and to expect to see progress.

If the owner has full confidence that the trainer and horse fit well together, then he should have full trust that the trainer will bring forth all that the horse is able to do. The trainer needs to have a completely free hand. The owner cannot tell the trainer how he should work the horse, nor set the schedule of training—Second Level by next Spring, etc. Many things arise in training that might be more or less difficult for the horse. If the earlier training has gone fluidly and easily, there is no guarantee that each new exercise will be just as easy. If the owner gives the trainer a time limit to get over those difficulties, then both trainer and horse will get nervous about the work, and pressure for success will arise that is never good for classical training.

Many owners are very successful in their personal lives and often expect the same from their horses, but this can only happen when horses and riders have enough time to get to their goals. From the rider's perspective, he is in it for the love of the sport and the horses. It is always tragic for a rider who has worked so hard with a horse, when the owner decides to sell because he is impatient with the slow progress, or on the other hand because the rider has been so successful that he sells the horse for a large profit.

Of course, the owner's responsibility is first and foremost to the horse, and this requires dedicated, if diplomatic, supervision of the overall progress of the training. The main thing to watch for is the harmony and fit between the trainer and horse. When this becomes lost, it is time to find a new trainer.

3.4 *The Owner as Boarder*

As we have discussed, once you become a horse owner, you have the responsibility to provide stabling, feed, water, and general boarding care for your horse. If you own your own farm, you will be able to control the quality of care and service as far as your budget will allow. Most horse owners are not so fortunate as to have their own farm, and therefore must secure the services of a boarding facility to house their horses.

There are many factors that enter into the choice of a boarding facility, and there is no perfect boarding situation. The challenge is to match your interests and needs as closely as possible to those provided by the barn. Here are some questions to consider:

Are you studying with a particular instructor? If so, you need to find a barn where this person will be welcome to teach. Not all barns welcome outside instructors, and not all instructors will travel to all barns. Be sure you, the instructor, and the stable management agree on the use of the facilities for instruction. Determine whether there would be an extra fee or restrictions on when you can have lessons.

Do you need more intensive instruction and help? First time horse owners or those moving up to a more advanced horse will often benefit from being at a barn with a large instructional and training program. Good instructors constantly have an eye on everyone riding in the arena, and can spot trouble before it develops too far. They can provide advice on more advanced aspects of horse care, or can be called upon for additional lessons. If you need help and you are in a quiet barn where there are no kids, no lessons—and no experienced professional instructor on hand at all times—you may well miss the help you need when you need it.

Is peace and quiet or camaraderie your goal? Some people look to horses for a chance to escape from the hectic pressures of the everyday world, commune with nature and build an individual bond with these magnificent (and mute) animals. These folks typically feel that they already have all that they need in the way of social interaction in their lives away from the barn, and don't need or want another source of human companionship while they are at the barn. Other people are naturally more gregarious, and see the barn as an extension of their other social activities. The stable becomes their country club. Boarding stables exist that can satisfy either type of person. Choose the stable that fits you.

Is your riding interest shared by others at the barn? Usually, a dressage rider will enjoy boarding at a barn with other dressage riders, just as a hunt seat rider would enjoy boarding with other hunt seat riders. Being the "odd man out" can be awkward at times. This principle is not absolute. In regions where there are not many dressage riders, for instance, the one "dressage barn" available in the area may be otherwise objectionable for any of the above reasons. You may well be happier at a barn with combined training riders, or jumpers, or western, or whatever.

Is the barn well managed, safe and affordable? By answering the above questions, hopefully you have found several places that provide a good fit and meet your needs. But most important is that the facility meets your horse's needs—safety, good care and good management. Things don't need to be fancy, but they should be clean, well organized and well maintained. If the barn, tack room, feed room, turn-out arrangements appear to be chaotic or neglected, chances are the care of your horse will be, too.

Running the boarding farm

Boarders need to remember that the boarding farm is managed and run by the owners of the farm, not the owners of the horses. When a boarder wants everything in the barn to be 100% to his own liking, then he should build his own.

When things are not to your liking, the only appropriate course of action is to speak with the stable owner or manager. If you see a problem, it is only reasonable to bring it to the attention of someone who can fix it. Many times, however, boarders prefer to just complain among themselves. This can produce an atmosphere of negativity that inevitably will affect and infect the horses who live there—and does nothing to fix the problem!

Very few boarding facilities are run as profit-oriented businesses. Frequently a horse owner builds a farm and then seeks boarders to help defray the costs. These farm owners are often professional people with other full-time jobs, who are trying to ride and compete their own horses, and in general are losing money on the farm and horses. This does not excuse them from keeping high standards of care, but it also does not free them up for extra hours of inspecting for trouble. The boarder who sees a problem and brings—calmly and discreetly—it to the owner's attention is doing everyone a big favor: the horses, the other riders, and the owner, too. A responsible barn owner will never object to being informed of a problem that needs attention— although he may object to the method and tone of delivery!

Boarders should also understand that stables are very labor-intensive operations. The cost of feed, bedding, hay, electricity, insurance, pest control and so on are considerable, but even more so is the cost of the labor needed to measure and dispense feed and supplements, administer medications, put on and take off blankets and boots, clean the stalls, store the hay, repair the facility, and so on. Boarders who want special treatments or services should be prepared to pay for it.

3.5 Summary

As the "Chairman of the Board," the owner has the very highest responsibility for everything that happens to the horse. He has to choose everything wisely, the horse, as well as the rider, trainer, stable manager or boarding farm. He must be vigilant that each member of our Circle of Trust plays his role in a constructive and positive way.

4

the rider

We now come to the two members of our Circle of Trust who have the most direct influence on the development of the horse: the rider and the trainer. But isn't the trainer the rider? Doesn't the rider train the horse? In many instances, this is true, but it need not be. Here we will separate "riding" from "training" by recognizing that the primary duty of the rider is to improve himself—become more skillful, more subtle, and develop better aids and attitude. The primary duty of the trainer is to improve the horse—we will come to him in the next chapter.

4.1 The Problem

To be a rider requires self-discipline and respect for the nature of the horse. Ultimately, the rider directs and controls the team, deciding upon the exercise or movement, perhaps adhering to the requirements of the prescribed test. But the best riders almost appear to have yielded control to the horse—the horse seems eager to perform the next movement of the test or the next exercise called for. How is this done? With great tact, better balance, extremely careful use of the aids, and a touch of cunning. A slight shift of the rider's balance, and the horse thinks he wants to go left, another and the horse thinks he might like to go right, another and the horse would like to canter, yet another and he thinks perhaps it's time to stop. You can imagine that such an attitude requires a lot of trust in the rider. The horse needs to be thinking of how well things are going, how good he feels, what fun it is to use his muscles this way, what a nice partner he has to play and dance with. You should also know that it requires a lot of trust on the part of the rider. She needs the balance and skill discussed above, but also the confidence that this method will work, and patience to let the idea occur to the horse. These last two come only through experience, developing balance and skill requires hard work.

It seems that one has to reach a certain age to realize how difficult riding really is. At first, people think riding is easy—you just hop on and ride. Then after the first lesson, they think it is impossible, dangerous and to be avoided. Then comes a bit of success, because it is the instructor's job to instill confidence, and make it easy for the horse and rider. Lessons are carefully constructed and exercises arranged to ensure success. But unfortunately, this success is often confused with wisdom. Over the years, the riders sometimes become over-confident in their own abilities, blaming difficulties on the poor horses. Eventually, they see the light and work hard to develop a solid understanding and an appropriate level of confidence and humility.

Learning is like rowing against the current:
The moment you stop, you shall regress.

Chinese proverb

If you stop learning, you will soon stop riding. You never learn everything, and nothing you learn applies the same to every horse, so if you don't continue to learn you will not be able to ride many horses. Like every human being, each horse is an individual who has to be handled accordingly. The good rider knows very early on what will work with each new horse she rides.

The best riders keep the well being of the horse as their highest priority. What does this mean? As a rider, one's first duty is to learn to sit well and to use the seat and aids with ease and tact. This takes time, and careful instruction, and is best done on the kindest and gentlest horses, the stoics of the horse world—dedicated school horses. As one's skill progresses, more advanced horses, with bigger movement will help, but you never really lose the need to work on refining and developing your seat.

The saddle has a very big influence on the comfort of the horse and the effectiveness of the rider. The first picture shows how a correctly fitting saddle puts the rider in a place where he can correctly influence the horse with his aids. The second picture shows a saddle that is too low in the front and too high in the back. This puts the rider in the fork seat. The third illustration shows a saddle that is too high in the front and too low in the back. This puts the rider in the chair seat. Saddle padding and horses' backs change over time, so the saddle fit should be checked regularly.

It is a shame to see so many poorly sitting riders. Whenever possible, do seat exercises on the lunge, so that someone can watch and help. When I was riding and competing in Germany, we always had to be corrected on the lunge once a week, no matter how well we were doing at the shows. It does not make any difference how advanced you are, small mistakes can creep in. This is even a problem for professional riders, who are constantly riding difficult horses. In fact, this can be an even bigger problem for them, because most of the time, no one will say anything to point out a mistake to these "big name" riders.

Patience and practice
The next duty to the horse is to develop patience. The rider must recognize when he has given improper aids (and strive not to do that again!), or when he is asking for

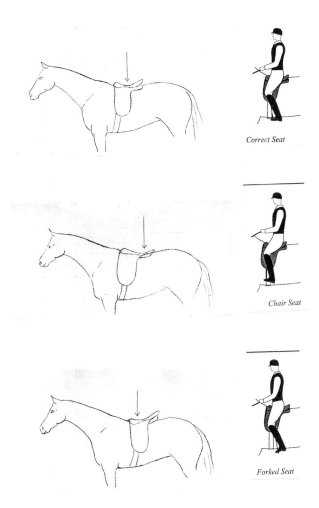

Correct Seat

Chair Seat

Forked Seat

something a little bit new from the horse. The rider should also know his own limitations, when to seek more expert advice and help, and how to take best advantage of that advice and help. This requires patience with yourself, as well as with your horse. I have seen many, many students who become upset at being unable to understand or do what I ask in a clinic. An instructor uses words to convey feelings, and perhaps the words are not chosen so well. Some give-and-take with the instructor may be needed to clarify what we mean. But even so, riding is not a theoretical activity. You have to train your body to perform the movements that you and your instructor have just discussed. Eventually, these movements become natural and you will not need to think the words and then perform the action—you act before thinking. This is what training yourself as a rider is all about. No amount of book reading alone can make this happen for you—it requires time in the saddle, patiently working through the words and ideas.

A very good, deep and long seat with discreet contact. Rider could carry hands a bit higher. Lisette Milner is the rider. Photo by Mark Neihart.

In Kronberg, Germany, a lady came to me for instruction and thought that because she had read everything Muesler ever wrote in his book **Reitlehre**, that I did not have anything to say to her that she did not already know. I thought to myself, "This could be fun!" Naturally, it did not go well. Even just walking on from the halt was no good. How could her poor horse know anything about Mueseler's theory? You only learn to ride by riding.

4.2 Goals of Good Riding

The horse is a fine, sensitive animal. Only when the rider applies the aids very carefully, in balance and at the right moment, can she feel how sensitively the horse reacts to the aids. The "correct" aids are best because they seem to speak the horse's language, i.e., they have the most natural and clear meaning to most horses, as learned over thousands of years of experience. The good rider knows that every aid she gives, every action she takes must be intentionally and specifically designed to reach the horse mentally as well as physically. She knows exactly what she can ask from her horse, and exactly where to stop.

When we listen carefully to what the horses have to tell us, we realize that "difficult horses" are often simply highly sensitive ones, who react quickly to many, many aids the rider is not yet familiar with. Perhaps the rider gives more aid than is needed or gives the aids in the wrong moment, and the horse surprises the rider with a sudden response. A very good rider will like this type of horse, because she will learn to give finer aids. Our failures with these horses are just a sign of a hole in our education. The true rider comes to the point where riding is a joy of discovery. Difficulties are not problems, but opportunities.

Some other horses will frustrate you and make you feel incompetent because they have been poorly trained, or do not recognize or listen to your aids. (A simple example is a Western pleasure horse trained to neck-rein with no contact.) His reactions are not what you expect. All the familiar aids you use seem not to work. You become stronger and repeat the same aids over, then stronger still. Imagine yourself in a foreign land where you do not speak the language. Someone says something to you that you do not understand. Since it is clear that you do not understand, the other person says the same gibberish again. Then again, but slower, then louder, and is finally shouting at you at an unbearably slow pace in a language that you have no way to understand! You get frustrated and give up on the communication. So it is with the horse: he will become frustrated, confused, and perhaps angry because he does not understand the rider's aids. He will become more frightened and the session will deteriorate. Sometimes, a horse will not pay attention, and a sharper aid might be needed for an instant, but the rider must determine very quickly whether you are both "speaking the same language." If not, you need to go right down to the basics, be very clear but soft with the aids, and find out what works, building confidence and comfort in the session.

4.3 *Extending your education*

In riding, we must use our head just as much as our seat, legs and hands. Lessons on a good horse with a good instructor are surely the time-honored way to learn riding, and I have already said that you need to learn riding by actually doing it. But when the rider sits down and reads, often she can more clearly see the point that the instructor was trying to make in a lesson. In the lesson, the instructor must make corrections and keep the session moving, and may not always have enough time to clarify all ideas. Reading gives the rider the time to reflect and relate theory to the practice of the recent lessons. It is most helpful if the instructor is aware of the material being studied, or even suggesting which books and articles to read. We had a saying: *Theory comes from the experience of the practice and is for the practice.*

Videotapes are another method to help riders improve. Whether watching videos of yourself riding or others, there are many things that you can learn. When you watch videos of your own riding, you can sometimes see what your instructor is talking about. Often a rider thinks his reins are short when they are not. No amount of instruction can seem to budge the rider's hands, until a video of her riding shows her how she is really doing things. Visualization based on watching others (pretending you are the much better rider whom you have observed), is very effective.

Do not ride only in lessons. Practice on your own, but be aware of the difference between lessons and riding by yourself. In a lesson, teachers can correct mistakes very early, because they see problems sooner than the rider feels them. The instructor can note the strengths and weaknesses of the student and can arrange the lesson accordingly. When you practice, be aware that things will not always go so smoothly. Many students try and practice the difficult, new things because they are exciting and give the impression of progress. But one should also practice those movements and aids that are going well in lessons. Remember that a good rider needs to have most everything happen almost automatically. They don't have to think, "keep your heels down," the heels just go down. But good riders were not born with reflexes that put their heels down. Long ago they struggled and concentrated on their heels and position until everything felt natural. So when practicing on your own, be sure to spend time confirming the things that go well in lessons. Put them into your collection of "instincts."

When taking lessons, it is important for the student to accept corrections, while always feeling for (and remembering) every good or bad reaction. In our Circle of Trust, the student must be able to trust her instructor, just as the teacher can also trust her. Instructors feel a responsibility to help the student get the most out of a lesson. They hope that every student comes out of the session with the feeling that he learnt something and with eager anticipation for the next session. This will be possible only if the student tries hard and has full confidence in the instructor. If the student does not have enough trust in the instructor to try hard to do what is being asked, she should find another instructor whom she will be more inspired to follow.

4.4 *Qualities of a good rider*

Kindness and self-control are the essential qualities of a rider. It is not sportsmanship to expect too much from the horse, and too little from the rider. Riders make mistakes. In every sporting activity, we make mistakes. In golf, bowling, tennis, or any other sport, we make mistakes and accept them for what they are—our mistakes, not the mistake of the ball. But in riding, we often blame the horse for our own failings. You have probably heard that riding is much more difficult than other sports because there are two separate conscious beings involved. This is true, but it does not lead to the conclusion that the horse is to blame—you cannot "blame" the horse for being stubborn, lazy, untalented or slightly lame. At a show, you can see three types of people: those who blame their horse, those who make excuses, and those who recognize just what a horse is, and accept imperfection.

When the rider keeps in mind that a horse is an animal, and cannot share the desires and aspirations of herself, she knows that the test will have flaws, but accepts them as part of riding. She can go over the test and see where she made mistakes and work to do better the next time, but she is clear that the horse did what was asked and what he was capable of. If the test had problems, the good rider questions what she did wrong. Was the warm-up hurried? Were aids given poorly? Was the rider mentally distracted? Was the horse entered at the wrong level? What can I do to improve?

Accepting mistakes is not an opening to make excuses. You can hear excuses outside any show ring. Instead of understanding the source of the problems, the rider "explains" the troubles by enumerating the shortcomings of the horse. It is the rider's disappointment that is showing. Excuses don't harm the horse, but they tell us that the rider is not thinking about what she needs to do to become better. The rider is not taking responsibility.

If you don't take responsibility, it is easy to go the next step and assign blame to the horse. I have seen riders come out of tests, go off to the side and spank their horse with the whip. They think the horse was malicious, and deserves punishment. Fortunately there are rules that try and control such outrageous behavior, but any rider who feels anger after a test is wrong. This is a sign of weakness or stupidity.

4.5 *Summary*

One is never finished learning, whether it is in life or especially in riding, where we have to bring two completely different natures together. More importantly than lessons, shows, clinics, video tapes and books, the best teachers are our horses. Their reactions to our aids let us know whether we have been clear, too rough, or ineffective, and let us know whether the aids were given in the right moment. These reactions are his language to tell us he did not understand the aids. We have to learn this language of our horses. Ears back, kicking, tail swishing, unsteady head movements, falling out of the hind legs in turns, and canter departures on the wrong lead are only some reactions used by the horse to tell us that it has not understood or at least misunderstood our aids.

In our Circle of Trust, the rider has the most direct influence on the performance of the horse. There are many products now being sold to make the horse more comfortable or perform better—-custom saddle pads, foams and gels, specially designed saddles, bridles and bits, special reins, exotic shoes, supplements and sports medicine treatments, and so on. They are all designed to make life easier and more comfortable for the horse, but not a one will protect the horse from bad riding. The Circle of Trust requires that the rider study and work hard to be the best she can be.

Next on our Circle is the trainer. Once armed with a good seat, quiet and effective aids, and excellent balance, the rider must become a trainer. To this point, we have thought of how to ride, next we will discuss what to ask the horse to do.

5

the trainer

The trainer's duty is to bring the horse to his highest potential through systematic development of balance, strength and cooperation with the rider. The rider's duty is to bring the seat and aids to the highest potential to work harmoniously with the horse. And the instructor is there to help the rider and trainer to become better at their work. I have discussed the rider, and will now discuss the roles of trainer, remembering that it is often the case that rider and trainer are the same person.

5.1 *The Goals of Training*

The goal of all training is to bring out the best in our horses. This includes the best physical condition, talent and attitude. Our joy and reward comes from the strengthening and deepening of our partnership with the horse in the daily work. A fundamental rule of training is that the horse must enjoy and look forward to his work. A good trainer learns to recognize the exact strength of each of his horses. He will keep his horses in top form for many years by taking the time to really build up the young, talented horses very carefully and calmly, forward and straight. We should not rush our horses from show to show to win as many ribbons as possible—the success and ribbons will be quickly forgotten. Even the best and the most willing horse will lose his potential sooner or later. Our duty is to take care of all our horses throughout their careers, and to be very gentle and kind to them even when they are no longer winning us ribbons and trophies.

A trainer is simply a rider who is working on improving her horse. So in some sense everyone becomes a trainer very early in their riding careers. One of the essential questions in training horses is "who trains the trainer?" How do we ensure that we don't just stumble through the process? The German national equestrian federation has a formal system for training the trainer, we will examine it next. Then we will discuss "riding to the limit, but not over the limit." This concept embodies my philosophy of responsible training. The training scale serves as guideposts along the way. Training to the limit, but not over does not mean that you can not get somewhere efficiently. In the section "Timelines for Training," I set out how an experienced trainer, with a capable young horse, bit of luck and a lot of dedication can bring a horse to Grand Prix.

5.2 *The German national instructor training system*

From 1928, when equestrian events were first included in the Olympic program, to the time of this writing, the Olympic Games have been held every four years except for during WWII, 1940 and 1944. Of these eighteen Olympic dressage events, ten were won by the German team. From 1966 to 1996, the German team won nine of the ten competitions, missing only the controversial Moscow Olympics, where the Russian team won. From 1963 to 1999, the German team won all eighteen world championships. Thus, no one can deny that Germany has consistently produced the best trained horses in the modern era. It will be useful therefore to examine its system for producing horse trainers.

A brief history

For those of us interested in horses and horse sport, the resurrection of the German sport horse program after its virtually complete destruction in WWII is a modern miracle. Before the war, breeding and training were largely dictated by the needs of the army or of thoroughbred racing. Horse shows were usually reserved for officers, and very few entries were accepted from civilian riders. [2] During the war, a few sport horses had been saved from the opposing armies, but this was rare.[3] The army's cadre of trained horsemen was decimated. The same was true for the poor horses. They suffered heavily, especially in the Russian war and later on by fleeing from East to West. Very few horses and trainers survived, but with those, the new program was begun. After the war *Oberlandstallmeister* Dr. Gustaf Rau took on the task of re-generating the German sport horse program. He recognized that any serious breeding and riding program would have to depend on the farmers, at least in the short run. Horses that performed farm-related chores from Monday to Friday, morn-

---

[2] An exception occurred during the 1928 Olympic Games in Amsterdam, where a civilian, Freiherr von Langen, won a gold medal with his horse Draufgaenger. Von Langen in fact had been an officer in the Cavalry but had to quit because of a serious injury in World War I.

[3] We must never forget all those who made unspeakable sacrifices for the riding sport and horse breeding. One of them was *Oberst* Podhajsky. He saved the horses of the Spanish *Hofreitschule* in Vienna from the Nazis who believed that the school was a waste of money that could be better used for the purchase of weapons and the bombing of the Allies. Later on, help came from the American General Patton who brought all breeding stock out of Czechoslovakia through the chaos at that time. After a long journey the horses were back home on their own breeding farm. Both of those gentlemen deserve our boundless gratitude.

As early as three years after the disastrous World War II, we had organized the first shows, like here in Heidelberg. Wearing the trench coat is Landstallmeister *Dr. Gustav Rau, the "re-generator" of the equestrian sport in Germany after WWII.*

This was the typical attire of these times, both for dressage and jumping. Notice the very few jackets. In 1948, after the cruel war, both sides were ready and willing to resume riding competitions and to put the ugly past behind them.

ing until night, were put in training on the weekends and began to take part in the first post-war shows. By 1948, barely three years after the end of the war, through the farmers' riding clubs and with the help of the American, French and British rider friends, we were able to organize our first shows.

These were some typical victory ceremonies. In 1950, when these photos were taken, things had begun to look a little better.

Venues, equipment and even riding attire were scarce, but the most important thing for us was that we could ride at shows again. We were all grateful that we could once again celebrate victory on show grounds, not on the battlefield. The riders had shared the bonds of equestrianism with so many good friends on both sides who did not come home from the war. They could never understand or accept why their friends and fellow competitors had become their enemies. Only politicians had asked for the war, which visited so much suffering and hardship on so many people.

Dr. Rau worked passionately to ensure that horses would remain a vital part of German life. He created the "Day of the Horse" as part of his strategy to re-generate interest in horses and horse sport. Riders got together for festivities in front of their town halls, and riding clubs held open house to bring the horse closer to the city people.

Soon riding clubs began to be started in the cities. Increased demand for horses created an incentive for the breeders to re-build their programs, and they began to produce fine horses. With the development of the industry, private stables grew and could have more and better horses that could be presented at shows of increasing quality. More and more members joined the clubs, which led to a shortage in trainers. Therefore, a systematic way of training instructors had to be developed. The survivors of the military—sergeants and officers, came through. They had never lost their love of the sport and started riding and teaching again. They formed the backbone of the effort to train professional teachers and riders, who were eventually united in a professional society, the *Federation Nationale*, or FN. Riding Master Festerling is the former president of the FN. As of this writing, that society has 730,000 registered members in 6,500 riding clubs within Germany. On the breeding side, there are 2,816 registered stallions and 37,079 mares in Germany, for a total of 39,895 warm blood horses. There are also 770 registered riding pony stallions and 7,825 pony mares, for a total of 8,595 riding ponies.

The German system of today

Today's German riding clubs and private stables may wish to become accredited as training facilities, with a professional teacher (*Reitlehrer*), qualified to prepare apprentices for the professional exams. In the modern system such accreditations, once approved by a committee consisting of a professional instructor, a representative of the Education Department and a government official, are administered by the FN. To obtain this certification and accept students, a facility needs a professional teacher, facilities and horses: It must have a 20 by 40m indoor riding arena, a 20 x 60m outdoor riding facility, a dressage and a jumping ring. It should also have a hacking trail.

Landstallmeister *Dr. Gustav Rau initiated the celebration of "The Day of the Horse" as a way to bring the horse closer to people at large. It was a "Day of Open Doors" in all riding clubs, as here in front of the Heidelberg City Hall in 1967.*

It must have experienced dressage and jumping horses along with young horses for the students to learn on. Housing and eating facilities for the students, and a schoolroom for theory classes are required. The training is to be equally thorough in dressage and jumping; there can be no specialization until the student has passed his first (*Bereiter*) exam, when he can choose to go to either a dressage or a jumping stable. Until that point, the student must become proficient in both.

The training of a *Bereiter*

The first certification a rider obtains is that of the *Bereiter* or professional rider. This training takes three years. After the first year, the students are be examined in Warendorf at the *Deutsche Reitschule* or at a recognized *Landesreitschulen*, to determine the candidate's suitability. If they are judged to be unsuitable, they will be told to look for a different profession. During this first year, they learn about stable management and work on developing their dressage and jumping skills. They also attend special classes to prepare them for the business aspects of the horse industry. They also get lunge lessons to develop correct seats. When possible, vaulting and gymnastic exercises on the lunge without saddle are also included in the training. In the second and third years of training, candidates learn how to ride dressage with snaffle and double bridles, and will continue to work on jumping, cross-country, lungeing and teaching skills.

The subjects that must be taught are regulated by the government. They are:

1. Horse care. Leading and transporting horses to shows, hunts or to the veterinary.

2. History and nature of the horse. Anatomy.

3. Health, hygiene and shoeing.

4. Exercising and working of school horses, as well as advanced horses in dressage, jumping and cross country.

5. Breeding and pedigrees. Breeds and the number of breeding farms and their locations.

6. Nutrition and growth. Use of different feeds; how much and often. Turn-out.

7. Keeping of horses and facility construction. Technical equipment.

8. Machinery and equipment operation and maintenance for keeping the arena and outside rings leveled.

9. How the training facility works as a business: purchasing the feed, collecting the riding fees, salaries for employees and time schedule for the riding lessons.

10. General laws as they pertain to equestrianism.

11. Industry and Society; riding clubs and FN rules.

12. First aid for horse and rider through clinics at the Red Cross and a veterinary.

13. Environmental science (nature and animal protection is very important in Germany).

Throughout the period at the training facility, the candidate has to keep a daily record in his journal, relating everything that was covered during the day. Once a month he has to write a special report on certain specified training and stable management topics. These reports must be presented at the exam and they are graded. There is a tremendous amount that an apprentice has to learn in the very short time of only three years. This is why teachers tend to select only apprentices who are already quite experienced in theory and riding. It reflects badly on the teacher if an apprentice does poorly on an exam.

At the end of three years, the candidate will undergo a two-day examination in Warendorf. Usually, there will be fifteen to twenty examiners from different locations, who stay in a nearby hotel. All expenses are paid by the riding clubs. A full day is taken up with a written exam covering theory and the thirteen subject areas above. On the following day, candidates are examined in teaching, lungeing, riding young and more experienced horses, up to the L Level in dressage (approximately 2nd Level in the US) and jumping fences up to 1.3 meters in height (approximately 3'9"), grooming and stable management.

Reitlehrer certification

A *Bereiter* may make a career of riding in private barns, showing horses for sponsors, or working for breeding farms. If he wishes to become a teacher, he has to be certified as a *Reitlehrer*, or professional teacher. He then must work two more years in his own or a new riding club under supervision of a professional teacher, and must train and compete a horse to 3rd level in dressage and jumping. He must also organize small shows and hunts, Christmas events, and club competitions. These activities are very important in keeping the club together and contribute to a good overall professional discipline.

The *Bereiter* also studies how to run the business and become qualified to stand in for the *Reitlehrer*. After two years he returns to Warendorf or another recognized school such as the Bavarian *Landesreitschule* for further preparation. After passing the exam, the candidate becomes a *Reitlehrer* and as such can teach professionally and assume the responsibility for a riding club. Most teachers work in riding clubs, where they have to teach dressage and jumping at all levels. Only very few actually work in private stables because most of those specialize either in dressage or jumping.

You can see how seriously the preparation and qualification of professional riders and teachers is taken in Germany. Nevertheless, I'm sad to say, even such careful preparation does not always ensure the integrity of the end result. For example, on the day of the *Bereiter* exam, the owners of dressage and jumping stables are already waiting, so they can hire the best *Bereiter* to train for them. Successful candidates get great offers, lots of money, room and board and very good and expensive horses to ride and show. This is of course great for those young people. Until now they had to work very hard riding and grooming and did not see too much money. They are very willing to say yes to these offers. However, this is when the "success pressure" starts for them, because the owners want to see success with their good and expensive horses after a reasonable period of time. The pressure for these young trainers is tremendous, who must now for the first time ride without the watchful eye of their own teachers, who would always keep them on the right path. On their own, these young trainers can become unsure, and mistakes creep in. They feel pressure to achieve quick successes with the very good horses entrusted to them for training. Whatever brings about this success most quickly may seem to be the right way. Unfortunately, rushing the horse will lead to a fight in most cases, because the young trainer asked too much too soon—before the horse was ready to cope physically and mentally.

5.3 Fundamentals: Dressage in Harmony

Take good care to choose the correct means, then the goal shall easily reveal itself.

Mahatma Gandhi

Remember "The Horse's Prayer" found on page 10. No trainer should ever forget the kindness, the generosity and the forgiving nature of our equine partners. In many stables you can see the horse's prayer posted, as a reminder of all of our obligations toward these selfless creatures.

I have presented the details of my training methods in my book **Dressage in Harmony**, which shows how to work in concert with this credo. Recently I received a call from a former student of mine who was very impressed with my book. But he asked why it was not published twenty years ago, when we could have led our riders on the right track. Of course he is right, but better late than never to help our horses and riders.

I am reminded of a comment by Gigi Nutter: "The most important lesson I received from Mr. Zettl was the word 'give'." It is so easy to take but so hard to give. This takes lots of self-control. The taking needs only strength and submissiveness of the horse.

Many people have commented that they are surprised at my teaching, because they associate German riding with force and very strong aids. For a time this was true. The August, 1983 issue of the German Dressage magazine, *St. Georg* reported on the European Dressage Championship: "The German riders could keep the domination, but the individual winner was Anne-Grethe Jensen with Marzog. This could show a new trend. Harmony and contentedness instead of force, strength and submissiveness." The success of the Danish pair was sensational. Marzog had 1501 points, Ahlerich 1365 points.

Lungeing, the first time the young horse is asked to go on a controlled circle.

After this my former boss and friend Hans Pracht said: "Walter, you are absolutely right with your philosophy and teaching. We all must more ride independent of our hands and softer with our aids." Not only Hans Pracht, the whole German riding world came to the conclusion that the training had to become softer. This was the influence of only one rider! This model of correct training, however, is under constant assault from the temptation to resort to short cuts, which do not require any self control and balance, only more strength.

Many up and coming riders do not like to follow the principles of classical training, because it takes much too much time and requires a lot of self discipline and patience. They resort to shortcuts to obtain rapid success. They have a stable full of horses, too many horses to allow a correct training for all. We witness a training style that sneaks in slowly but steadily, which does not make our horse our partner but makes the horse obedient through excessively rough riding, ultimately creating bitterness and unhappiness for both horse and rider. Having a very talented horse in his barn should make every rider happy. This talent, as well as his impressive gaits and good looks, however, can often lead to the temptation to push him ahead too quickly. This puts the horse "over his limit."

It is the horse who teaches the rider how he should act. He shows what he would like to tell the rider—that he is happy or uneasy—by volunteering special movement or little resistances. This is the horse's language that we must learn. Then we can develop a harmonious partnership that is built upon mutual respect. The horse will develop confidence in his rider, and accept guidance while remaining happy in his work. When the rider/trainer does not listen to these signs, or tries to "push through" problems, the horse does not develop, but loses confidence in the rider. This develops more resistance and can lead quickly to a horse becoming a fighter.

Natural instinct vs. machines

At the beginning of the training, the horse must go through a period of building trust in the rider, whom he should respect but never fear. Working only with the movements that the horse does naturally in the wild, the trainer makes these movements more brilliant and brings them under control, so they can be called on at any time. Under no circumstances may the trainer resort to uncontrolled force. The horse should do everything of his own will and every difficult exercise should be made easy. Every exercise should transition seamlessly into the next, because the trainer understands how to bring the horse slowly and incrementally from what he understands and can do, to the next level of difficulty. This enables the horse to comprehend and perform without needless mental or physical stress. For example: transition from a 20m circle (where the horse is bent for shoulder-fore), into a 10m circle, with the natural bending for shoulder-in to shoulder-in. Transition out of a 6m volte, with the natural bending for travers, into an actual travers. Transition from a collecting trot to a medium or extended trot. Transition from half step trot to an eventual piaffe or passage. Transition out of shoulder-in to a half-pass, or from a volte to a pirouette etc. This shows how we can move from a relatively easy exercise to the more difficult exercises.

Cavaletti are a great help for developing balance and relaxation in the walk...

...as well as the trot. Both photos by Jane Casnellie.

This can only work if we give the basic exercises enough time to build strength and comprehension. In this way muscles, bone structure, ankles, tendons, heart and lungs get strong and the horse attains the highest degree of training without losing relaxation and brilliance. When this is done correctly, none of the Grand Prix movements will be difficult for the horse. The horse learns to do the exercises almost without realizing the difficulty.

Throughout, it is important that we make different patterns and rhythms part of each training session and do not drill the horse. As far back as the fifties Erich Klahn reminded the riders in his book ***Dressur am Scheideweg*** (*Dressage at Crossroads*) that mechanical drilling only creates unnatural gaits and takes the pride and beauty of the horse away. The training should vary, including lungeing, cavaletti work, small jumps, and hacking; working up to jumping, three-day-eventing, and hunting in the fall. We never should turn our horses into dressage or jumping machines, where all movements and exercises look mechanical. This is what I call "poodle dressage."

5.4 To the Limit, Not Over

I have been thinking about how to help most people understand the concept of Dressage in Harmony, and what is a key guiding principle for training in harmony. I think that "to the limit, but not over the limit" is a nice expression that sums up the nature of training, and shows us how and when things can go wrong.

Riding "to the limit" is a narrow road to success. On the one hand, we have riding under the limit—this leads to under achievement and not reaching our goals. On the other hand, riding "over the limit" leads to disaster. Let's consider in turn what comes from riding to the limit, riding under the limit, and riding over the limit.

To the limit

Riding to the limit brings out strength, confidence, relaxation, fun, brilliance and harmony in the horse.

Strength. The progressive and careful development of the horse to his natural limit develops muscles, tendons, joints, and good lung and heart functions. Strength is a requirement for harmony, brilliance, confidence—and fun.

Confidence. Maintaining this confidence in his own strength and ability is key to a good partnership with our horse. Once lost, it is very difficult to restore this confidence. Riding to the limit builds each new challenge squarely on the foundation of the last. When the horse is introduced to new experiences gradually and carefully, he learns new things with confidence. Each new movement can cause apprehension in the horse. Riding to the limit takes the horse to this new ground, but familiar territory is only a short distance away, and the trainer can reassure the horse quickly and easily. Those riding under the limit may never touch newer movements, those riding over the limit frighten the horse by jumping to new movements without proper preparation.

Hunting in the fall. The author on the left, riding the thoroughbred mare Sprinterin in a nice manner.

Linda and Pat Parelli demonstrate the lack of use of a bridle or "traditional" aids from the hands with their two horses, Remmer and Magic. Linda's medium canter is beautifully relaxed, powerful and in perfect balance. Pat demonstrates an effortless and confident collection into piaffe. It is easy to recognize the fun horse and rider are having together, bareback and without a bit. Photo of Linda on Remmer by Coco. Photo of Pat on Magic by Molly Moore.

This confidence extends to the horse's own balance. Our horses are naturally balanced. With the weight of saddle and rider, however, the horse must find his balance anew every day, regardless of how advanced it is. The neck, which is the horse's "balance pole," must not be excessively shortened, so as not to interfere with the horse's natural ability to maintain his balance

Because the horse is a flight animal, he should always be given the feeling that fleeing to safety is an option. This is achieved by not holding him too tight with the hands. The rider's hands need to be soft and always ready to go forward. This builds up the horse's confidence in his own strength.

Relaxation. Riding "to the limit" includes relaxed movement. As soon as relaxation is lost and tension appears, we have crossed the line and are "Over the Limit." It is much easier to relax when you are strong and confident! A good relaxation should be recognizable in every exercise and gait, all the way to the Grand Prix level. This will make the whole process a lot easier for the horse and also eliminate the danger of wearing the horse out too soon.

Muscles must, of course, tense to support and propel, but then must relax immediately. Picture Fred Astaire, and how he relaxed the muscles that he was not using at any given moment. Each muscle has to be active when it is needed, but ready to relax in an instant. Slow-motion videos of Olympic sprinters show very clearly how the muscles relax very quickly— relaxed when they are in the air, but click in immediately when they are landing, ready to push off again.

The importance of relaxation has been recognized by other disciplines. During a recent visit with Linda and Pat Parelli, I was able to observe their relaxed way of training, which they call "Natural Horsemanship." Riders are shown how to teach the horse to get used to ourselves and our aids. With a lot of calmness, patience, and without any roughness, by playing games, the horses are taught to lose their fear and to develop trust in humans.

Brilliance. When the horse is strong and relaxed, and confident in his balance, he can let himself fly through the air, maximizing his athleticism, and not worry that he will fall or stumble or pull a tendon. Horses in nature love to show off their power and beauty. In every step we can easily see whether a horse has confidence in himself and his rider or whether this confidence has been lost.

Fun. A horse that is strong, relaxed and confident in his balance can enjoy and look forward to his work. The rider should always feel that judges and spectators alike notice that the horse has fun with the exercises and gets more beautiful and more proud.

A horse with average abilities can be turned into a super horse with a lot of patience and correct training. It is equally true, however, that a super horse can be degraded to an average one through incorrect training. All too often riders use aids

Horse and rider are in full harmony during this turn. Paul Schopf and Hawkeye. Photo courtesy of Susan Sexton.

that are exaggerated or too strong, holding the horse together and preventing him from really expressing himself in harmony with the rider's intentions and showing his brilliance. We have to show the horse what we would like to do, but we also must actually allow the horse to do it. By getting softer with the hand and the other aids you reduce them to the minimum necessary. In that way, the horse can enjoy working together with you.

Harmony. Appropriate control, strength, relaxation and confidence fuse into harmony—like ballet dancing. Two different beings, with completely different bodies and souls are molded together into one unit in full harmony, without any force. One exercise flows harmoniously into the next, without losing the rhythm and tempo.

Under the limit

Riding under the limit is not so very bad. Millions of riders who practice it, knowingly or unknowingly, get great satisfaction and have a loving relationship with their horses. They are afraid to ask too much because they never want to even think of going over the limit and doing harm to their horses. They need instruction that takes them closer to the limit and shows them where they can go, but they don't need instructors who push them over the limit. Their concern and love of their horses deserve our most profound respect.

More serious trainers can also miss many opportunities by not riding to the limit. They confuse light aids with lack of power, engagement, movement, and proper connection to the hand. We do not really do our horses any favors by not reaching a little more for the limit.

Weakness. By not exercising enough, the horse does not develop enough strength and musculature, and can be more likely to have joint problems and soreness. We know all too well that an insufficiently trained body is more susceptible to sickness and lameness. We know that more difficult movements require a lot of strength from the horse. Your horse might be mentally ready to move on to a more complex movement, but not strong enough to make it physically easy. To introduce the movement now requires challenging the horse mentally and physically, doubling the difficulty.

Unsure. Horses ridden under the limit are not naturally confident in their balance. They tend to keep their feet close to the ground and lose the good quality in the walk, trot, and canter.

Shuffling, stiff and flat movement. Weak and earth-bound gaits give the rider a soft feeling but make it impossible for the horse to be truly supple. Every movement and exercise will remain flat and powerless and miss spark and brilliance. Beginning riders often find these kinds of horses to have very comfortable trots, because there is no movement and little power. The aids can be very light, because nothing is ever asked for.

Dullness. The horses are asked to "behave," and signs of the horse having fun are cause for great worry. The horse is not encouraged to develop and express his athleticism.

The horse as a pet. Such a horse cannot perform Dressage in Harmony because of his lack of strength, confidence and suppleness. Nevertheless, he can be a very trusting, reliable companion.

Over the limit

Riding over the limit is the greatest source of trouble in training. Over the limit can mean too much work, too much stress, overly difficult movements practiced too early. The limit is mental as well as physical, and the good trainer is aware of his horse's attitude as well as his physical condition.

Over the strength limit. Pushing too hard can easily lead to all sorts of soreness, lameness, aches and pains of both soul and body. The training must be appropriate for the goal: you don't spend hours in the weight lifting room if you are planning on running a marathon.

Losing confidence. Any soreness or stiffness will cause the horse to worry. Exaggeration of the aids and demanding too much will make the horse afraid of the work and destroy his confidence in the rider and himself.

Tightness. Tightness is the result of trying to force the horse into an unnatural frame through too much force and an inflexible hand. The horse gets fussy and tight in his mouth. He opens his mouth, takes the tongue over the bit or lets it hang out. The horse does not step into the rider's contact with confidence, because he is too busy with his mouth, trying to rid himself of the strong rein aids. One muscle is tightened against the other. The jaw locks up and the neck becomes stiff. This leads to pain and resistance. A short neck blocks the shoulder, which in turn does not allow the hind leg to step under to make the muscles stronger and develop them more. This proper

Mary Claeys demonstrates the Spanish Walk. This is what we do not want to see in dressage. Photo by Paul Roach.

development is necessary so that we can send the *Schwung*, which was created by a more engaged hind leg, over a swinging back to the soft receiving hand. This allows the horse to automatically attain a correct elevation. A lack of correct elevation leads to soreness in the back, which shows up as a pacing walk, Spanish walk, tightness, short steps, fidgeting or marching.

Sourness and resistance. When horses are forced to go along with strong aids, they become less and less sensitive and will react only to stronger and stronger aids. They will not do anything willingly but will instead fight and resist to avoid the pain.

This will happen also when the horse is constantly nagged at. It is better always to ride with a focus on improving the next stride with a better aid or exercise, rather than trying to react or correct the last stride. It is, in fact, impossible for the rider to influence the stride he is sitting on at that moment. Everything about that stride was fixed and determined before it began. Attempting to address it will only make the horse confused and sour. The rider must always concentrate his effort on shaping and influencing the next stride.

Mechanical movement. Because horses that are ridden over the limit lose confidence in their ability to perform, movements are learned like tricks, as in the circus (what I call poodle dressage). All movements get stiff; transitions are not seamless but become abrupt instead. The half and full halt are not accepted willingly through the full body. They get blocked in the second or third vertebra, and the nose gets behind the vertical. The hind legs do not get lower. They do not carry, but only push. There is no self carriage and no relative elevation.

How to recognize riding over the limit at home

Riding Master Eggert confided in me that he once had a horse that was resistant. He felt he had to make the horse obey and spent 2½ hours to "correct" the horse. Instead of getting better, the horse got worse, the rider got frustrated, and finally gave up! The next day, the horse refused to go into the arena—sure, that he would find a maniac in there! He came to understand that this was not the right way, and that what is not obtained today will come tomorrow or next week or next month. What is done in force will never be good.

Riding over the limit is like a disease with many possible symptoms. They may all appear, or more likely, only some will show up. The presence of some of these symptoms is a cause for further diagnostic inquiry. The presence of all of them is a fair basis for a positive diagnosis. But the important thing is that the trainer be alert to their appearance and the possible trouble they signal.

Not going forward. Lazy or stubborn horses who are subjected to too much leg and spur aids will do exactly the opposite of what the rider intends. They will go even slower, because the excessive use kills the aids. Although it sounds paradoxical, these horses have to be driven with very little driving aids.

Let me tell you a story about myself. We got a very lazy horse in training once. I thought I should use the sharpest spurs. My old master took my spurs away. He told me I drive too much. He said "Only drive very little, do not drop your reins, keep a quiet, gentle contact to the mouth." To my surprise, after 20 minutes controlling myself like I never did before, this lazy horse that never liked to go forward for me suddenly went into overdrive and I had trouble controlling him. From this experience I saw how careful one has to be with the driving aids, which must always be in a fine balance. We always have to remind ourselves that our horse is a fine musical instrument like a violin that responds to the softest touch.

Kicking against leg and spurs. Throwing himself against the leg is a way to fight for horses with very strong characters. Sometimes these horses will lean a long time against the wall and almost crush the rider's leg. In the worst case the horse lies down and refuses to get up. I once had such a strong-headed horse in our barn to correct. The owner told me that using strong whip aids on this mare to make her obedient would make her lie down and shut off. With lots of love and patience the horse quickly got used to my aids, became more confident and began to react to and to respect just a light touch of the whip. Also, the horse did not hide any more in the farthest corner of the stall when she heard somebody coming, and started to trust the people again.

Because of bad experiences in her past, White Lady, here ridden by the author, attempts to escape the rider's aids by rearing and Lancades. Photo by Dr. Christiane Hebel.

Not standing still. If the rider tries to force the horse with excessively strong aids to stay still, the horse will get frightened, tense, and will struggle to move on. Many times this type of horse will start to throw his front legs into the ground and even will try to throw himself onto the ground. He tries to jump away in *Lancades* (the horse stands up on his hind legs and pushes himself very strongly forward), *Courbette* or stubbornly runs backwards. Both behaviors can be very dangerous because the horse is very frightened and in panic. He could run into a wall or anything that is in his way, or fall over. When horses have learned to do this, only a lot of patience, very careful aids, especially quiet and soft hands, a quiet, soothing voice, and with much luck will the horse slowly and quietly learn to stay still.

Rearing. Through excessive aids with hands, spurs and whip the horse's escape route has been blocked, and rearing becomes his only way out. The horse can throw himself backwards and fall on the rider.

Rearing can only be corrected through forward riding with a very experienced rider. Otherwise, the horse will panic and flee to get rid of the pain.

Teeth grinding. This is also the result of an excessively strong hand. The horse will fight against it and cramp up, developing incorrect musculature in his neck. The neck muscles should be most developed close to the shoulder and not on the small part of the neck nearest the poll. He is not stepping into the hand contact with confidence. Grinding is always very hard to correct and can become a bad habit. With the return of the slightest tightness, he will grind the teeth again.

Tail swishing. Mares or sensitive horses may develop this habit because of weakness in the back, or from a poorly fitting saddle that leads to a wrong seat and bad aids. Another cause is unquiet legs and spurs being used too far back. This is always a sign of unhappiness and pain (unless the horse has worms).

Ears back. This is also a reaction to excessively strong aids and weakness in the back, which results in unwillingness to work.

Throwing back of the head, snatching and rooting. These behaviors show lack of confidence in the hand of the rider, who tries too much to hold the horse in a frame. The horse tries to escape the excessive hand aids. A tilting of the neck, with one ear higher than the other and the nose too much to one side, is a sign that the rider is too strong with his hand.

Tongue and mouth problems. Horses with a sensitive mouth and riders with overly strong and unquiet hands can lead to tongue and mouth problems. The horse opens his mouth or pulls his tongue up, puts it over the bit or even lets it hang out of the side of the mouth where he is more tight and stiff. The horse uses his tongue as a pillow to soften the effect of the bit and rein. This can become a really bad habit. Problems in the mouth are very hard to correct and require a lot of time and even more patience, with a steady, quiet, soft and giving hand, especially on the tight rein. We have to get the horse away from too much pressure on this side and obtain more contact on the soft side. However, the horse will fall immediately back into this bad habit if the rider gets tight again. Making the nose band tighter and tighter will not cure the problem, and will only make the poor horse more uncomfortable and unable to focus on anything but trying to fight against this restriction on his ability to swallow and breathe.

Evading the aids through swinging the haunches in and out. This can be a problem with very sensitive horses, who are reacting too much to the rider's weight shifts and leg aids. Mares tend to do this especially. Every leg aid has to be light and must be accompanied by the opposite rein. This is especially important when teaching the flying changes, piaffe and passage. The horse must really be between both seat bones. The horse will escape aids that are not balanced, especially during flying changes, piaffe and passage. Instead of stepping under with the hind leg, he swings to the left and to the right. Regardless of the exercise, whether it is forward, lateral or backward, the door in the front must always remain open. Otherwise the hindquarter will have to go to the side. This type of horse should be ridden without spurs, yet always with a good, steady *Schwung* forward, without rushing.

Sweating due to fear. The sweat is not warm; it is cold. Many times the horse will dry off after a long cool down walk, but the sweat breaks out again in the stall. This results when the horse is weak, i.e., not physically and mentally fit: there has been insufficient conditioning for demanding exercises; the horse tires quickly; the rider begins to use stronger and stronger aids and the horse becomes afraid. All this will quickly result in fear-induced sweating. Such a horse must be built up again very slowly and carefully, both physically and mentally.

Soreness. Riding the horse over the limit includes not only riding with excessively strong and rough aids, but also allowing the horse to become sore due to poorly fitting tack or bad shoeing, sitting with too much weight on one side, pulling too much on one rein (rein lameness), too strong and long training, and insufficient rest periods.

Not dropping manure, not blowing. This can be a sign of tightness and lack of relaxation in the horse's internal organs and holding his breath. This could eventually result in weakness of the lungs and heart. These physical manifestations of stress can lead to colic or ulcers.

How to recognize a horse that is ridden over the limit at shows

When visiting the show grounds, you can observe the effects of riding over the limit. Often, there is no correct clear four beat walk. The movement is stiff. The medium and extended walk not shown at all.

The neck is short. The horse gets behind the bit and escapes the aids. There is no change in frame between collected, medium and extended gaits. The horse cannot stretch forward when the reins are offered, and cannot demonstrate self-carriage in *überstreichen*.

The horse is not in balance and has difficulty with shoulder-in, half pass and all lateral work. Everything is stiff and tight. The horse steps back or cannot stay absolutely immobile, squarely on all four legs in the halt.

He fails to cover ground in medium and extended gaits—he is a leg-mover, not a back-mover. This means that his legs swing forward, but the back is tight and does not swing.

There is no collected trot because of tightness. Instead, the horse only offers passage-like steps. In an attempt to avoid this mistake, the rider shows only working trot. Medium and extended trot can only be good if the collection is correct. Consequently, in medium or extended trot, this leg mover throws his front legs too high, slapping them back to the ground where the nose points because the neck is shortened and the nose pulled in. The hind legs struggle to keep the horse in balance and stay very close to the ground. Hence, the horse does not cover ground. The piaffe and passage are mechanical and there is no piaffe-passage transition (the horse remains stuck in piaffe). The rider does not sit quietly, but bounces up and down, hoping that the horse will cause the horse to offer a better piaffe. Instead, the horse feels pain in his back and gets tight. The leg of the rider is too far back and is not driving in the right moment, and the piaffe steps are too fast. Due to the excessive contact used to initiate this exercise, to pulling to the left and to the right with the hands, and to excessive lateral body movements by the rider, we observe the crossing of either the front or the hind legs, very wide stance to maintain balance, or the hind legs lifting higher than the front legs, because the horse does not have any possibility to step under and forwards. Here again the Schwung is lost.

The halts are not quiet, or don't happen at all, because the rider has not take the time to pay enough attention to the halt as an exercise, or has made the horse so tense in general that he is unable to relax even when he is standing still. The halt is the first and last impression of the judges in a test, and show a great deal about the quality and correctness of the horse's training.

There is kicking out, rearing, stopping in the test, shying, heavy sweating, and so on. These signs of resistance are easy to see, and clearly demonstrate that the relaxation, confidence, and harmony between rider and horse have been lost.

5.5 *The Training Scale*

It can be very hard to find the right path that allows the horse and rider not only to have fun in the work but also to get somewhere. For guidance, trainers can rely upon the training scale.

1. Rhythm. As in music, rhythm refers to the temporal sequence of beats-the four-beat pattern of the walk, the two-beat pattern of the trot, and the three-beat pattern of the canter. The rhythm of the gaits must be regular and even. Rhythm is closely related to relaxation in that lack of regularity is a sure sign of loss of relaxation. The rate at which the rhythm of each gait is repeated is the tempo. The rider must seek out and find the proper tempo for each gait for each horse. When the rhythm is rushed, the horse loses his balance and relaxation. We seek out a clear rhythm early in a horse's training yet have to pay constant attention to the regularity of the rhythm all the way through the training.

2. Relaxation. A relaxed horse is not stiff, not tight, not frightened. There is the obvious relaxation of the free walk on a long rein or a long, stretching trot, but there is also relaxation in action: a pirouette, passage or piaffe can either be tense or relaxed. Only when relaxed will the horse show brilliance in the movement. Muscles are found in extensor-flexor pairs and a relaxed horse tends to contract one or the other to achieve the desired movement of the limbs. A tense, nervous horse contracts both extensor and flexor muscles at the same time, thereby tightening and stiffening the joints through the action of the opposing forces. A truly relaxed horse will have every muscle relaxed from the poll to the tail, moving in regular rhythm and responding easily to all aids, and the hoofprints are light. The rider can take up the reins or give the reins, and the horse will maintain his rhythm without running away. This must be true of all three gaits.

3. Contact. Contact is the connection between the rider's hand and the horse's mouth. It lies at the center of our ability to control and communicate with the horse. For training we need very precise and responsive controls. It requires that the reins remain straight so they can instantaneously transmit increases or decreases in tension in the rider or the horse, and it requires that the horse's mouth remain soft, closed, and relaxed. The must go confidently to the bit, seeking the rider's hand contact. Contact is needed to balance the horse, keep him supple, regulate the impulsion, straighten the horse, guide the turns, and to collect. True contact must come from the activating and allowing seat and leg aids, not a pulling with the hand. The horse will readily pull back against a pulling hand, and the communication is lost when the horse locks the jaw and ignores any subtlety the rider may be trying to achieve through the hand. "Chewing the bit" is a common expression used to describe the soft connection desired in the horse's mouth. It does not mean gnashing with the teeth or opening the mouth. A proper contact does not require a flash or dropped noseband to hold the mouth closed.

4. *Schwung* describes the power of the hindquarters that carries the horse forward and its transmission over the back. Expression of this power requires an engaged, active hind leg and the release of the propulsive energy over the back, withers, neck, poll, mouth, and back to the receiving influence of the rider's hands. The closely related term, engagement of the hind leg, refers to the articulation of the joints of the hind leg, which like a spring gives more energy the more it is compressed. As relaxation and rhythm are the mental prerequisites for work, schwung is the physical prerequisite. Only when the horse has schwung can one ride in relaxed rhythm, with contact, suppleness, straightness, and collection. There can be schwung without collection, but never collection without schwung.

5. **Straightness.** The concept of straightness refers to the evenness of the horse from side to side. Although the horse's skeleton is symmetric, the horse is by nature one-sided (as people are right- or left-handed). The asymmetric development of muscles leads to a crookedness that inhibits the full performance of the horse. We see this in the typical situation where one side of the horse is much stiffer than the other. Thus movements such as canter, travers, half pass are easier to one side than the other. Through our training we aim to gradually bring the horse into more and more evenness on both sides. Only when the horse is straight is he able to perform every movement and figure correctly.

6. **Suppleness.** The power of the hind leg and control through the weight, legs, and hand will come to work against the rider's aims unless the horse is willing and able to flex and to readily follow the directives of the rider. Elastic, obedient fluidity of movement is the essence of suppleness, whether expressed through a supple back that transmits the power of the hind leg forward, or a softness to lateral bending that allows the horse to effortlessly flow from one small figure to another. The horse must be always ready to go forward, sideways or backward and all turns must be made without resistance. In other words, the horse should respond easily to all the rider's aids.

7. **Collection.** Collection is the highest step in our staircase of training. It is built squarely on the foundations of the previous six elements, since to a major extent it represents the distillation of the previous elements into a concentrated expression of the greatest harmony between horse and rider. It involves the lowering and increased engagement of the hindquarters that allow them to come more forward and

The foal Fotogenic. Photo by Jo-Anne Young.

under the weight of the rider. This elevates and lightens the forehand and makes possible the seemingly effortless execution of the smallest school figures or the brilliant extended movements. As the rider gains the feeling of riding more and more uphill, the end result will be both horse and rider truly in heaven.

Different writers may present these elements in a slightly different order, but that is because they are really quite strongly intertwined. As we develop contact and schwung, the horse gains balance and confidence, and the rhythm and relaxation will improve, as we develop better suppleness, the contact will become more sure and the rhythm clearer, as we develop better straightness, suppleness and schwung will improve. But the order is not entirely arbitrary. It is clearly wrong to demand straightness from a young horse without first establishing rhythm and relaxation, and it is not wise to ask for too much contact without relaxation.

5.6 Timelines for Training

There is a time for everything also means that everything needs time.

Ernst Ferstl

Let me answer one of the questions that I get asked the most often: How long does it take to get a horse to Grand Prix? The answer to this question comes in two parts: first, when do we start and, second, what happens along the way to the Grand Prix?

The Grand Prix work starts with the young foal, who must trust the handler, especially in the basic work. Any mistake made in the basics is hard to correct. This cannot be overemphasized.

Above: *Dr. Christiane Hebel on Wienerwalzer, riding in perfect harmony. Photo by the author.*

Left: *Free walk with long reins. Diane Creech on her horse Cantendar. Photo by the author.*

Once started into regular training, with a very good combination of a talented horse, rider and teacher, it will take around 4 years until the horse knows all the movements of the Grand Prix, if the training scale is adhered to. Then it will take another year to get everything together in test form. This timeline is only useful when everything goes as planned and difficulties that arise are corrected purposefully and skillfully without frightening the horse.

Year 1

In the first year we start the basic exercises. The horse should be no younger than 3½ years. The goal at this time is to build up the horse's confidence in the rider, and to develop a partnership. The horse needs to get used to the unfamiliar bridle, saddle, and rider. The first year of the training should be a confidence-building period. Here we build the foundation for a good or a bad training. What one does wrong in the beginning one can never fully correct later on. These mistakes are carried through the whole training, thus opening up the way for more mistakes.

The author on the horse Lustspiel
in a quiet halt, relaxed with gentle
contact, and patting the horse.

A young horse will sometimes try to get free of the unnatural weight of the rider
by bucking and running away. For the poor horse we can seem like a predator who has
jumped on his back. Through his youthful and sometimes unbalanced behavior, he
can easily hurt himself and should always have all four legs bandaged. Bandages
should not be too tight and removed immediately after the riding. This may not be as
necessary with an older and experienced horse, because he has his legs more under
control and is more in balance.

Especially when mounting, the horse should stand still in a quiet halt until the
rider gives the aids to walk on. This is the easiest and fastest way for the horse to get
his balance back. Horses are in balance in nature, but this balance gets lost as soon as
they are asked to carry saddle and rider. In the halt, the rider should correct his horse
very little, or not at all. When the rider corrects too much in the halt, the horse
becomes unsettled and is always waiting for the next correction. He never has the possibility to find his balance in the halt. After one year the horse will figure out how to
stay absolutely in balance and quiet.

In the walk, which is the most difficult gait, you should ask for as little as possible, because asking for too much too early in the walk can destroy this basic gait very
quickly. Through riding long, low and forward, with a very soft hand, the walk will
improve, the horse will trust your hand more, and he will step freely into the hand.
Ride a free walk on a long or loose rein, depending on the temperament of the horse.

Theresa Doherty in posting trot. The rider rises only slightly above the saddle. Horse and rider are in harmony and balance. Photo by Jane Casnellie.

The mouth and the back of the horse are the most sensitive parts and we have to do everything to keep this sensitivity. If we use too much hand the horse will soon start to make trouble by opening his mouth, letting his tongue hang out or over the bit. If the horse develops these problems, it is very time consuming to regain the trust in the rider's hand. When the back muscles are not developed correctly, the lightest weight will be too much and will cause the horse lots of pain.

The horse should be ridden away from the tight rein and encouraged to step towards the soft rein so he will start to straighten himself out. Trot in a good, correct rhythm, adapted to each individual horse, mainly on straight lines and large circles. The rider should post, so that the back of the young horse can begin to slowly develop muscles, allowing him to carry the rider without pain. The contact and frame should be long and low, so the horse is encouraged to stretch to the rider's hand. This complete willingness to stretch to the hand is a necessary first step to developing the half halt.

I would like to warn against beginning canter work too soon with young horses. With each canter stride, the horse has to transfer all his weight on to the outside hind leg, and then must use it to push his whole body up off the ground. Then, in the third beat of the canter, all his weight lands on the inside fore leg, which must now not only carry the whole weight of horse and rider, but also must initiate the suspension for the next stride. This explains how difficult it is for a young horse to remain in balance and how hard it is on his still weak bones, ankles and tendons. It takes at least a whole year for a young or inexperienced horse to develop a correct bone structure and musculature, especially in his back, tendons, joints, heart and lungs. He also has to develop confidence in the rider's hands, weight and aids. One must have the courage to take the necessary time, by keeping the horse at walk and trot for weeks and even months, until the balance necessary for a good canter has been achieved.

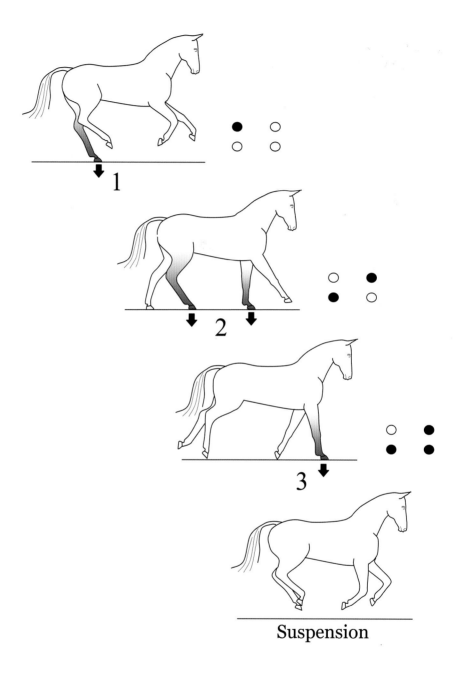

1

2

3

Suspension

Illustration of the canter footfalls by Professor Paul Schopf.

At this time it is especially unwise to school canter transitions. Because the young horse lacks the strength and balance to push himself and the rider up into a calm and balanced depart, most of the time when asked for the canter the horse, scrambling to comply, will throw even the best rider somewhat out of balance. This will make the young horse afraid of the canter, and that will take a long time for him to overcome. Future departs will be tense, anxious and rushed. It is much better to wait to school canter departs until the horse can produce a walk to trot transition that is consistently straight, powerful and precise. Of course, if the horse volunteers the canter, the trainer should ride it forward in a light seat. These volunteer canter departs are usually well balanced. One way to school the young horse in the canter without schooling the departs is to have him follow a trained horse, in the school or on a hack. When the experienced horse begins the canter, the young horse will usually follow suit.

It is especially important not to canter in too much collection and for too long, (even with an experienced horse, for that matter). Ride forward to create enough *Schwung*, which is indispensable to achieve good collection. A collected canter is very hard for the horse.

Toward the end of this first year, one can begin working on trot-canter transitions, leg-yielding, turns on the forehand, and lengthening in trot.

Through turning on the forehand and leg-yielding the young horse will learn to respect the lateral driving leg. This is also a very good exercise for the rider, as he must balance his aids.

Leg yielding, turn on the forehand: In order to accustom the horse to the stronger lateral aids involved in leg-yields, a left turn on the forehand may be indicated, immediately followed by a leg-yield right. The rider is Kim Anderson on her horse Laudable.

Above: Eddo Hoekstra on Rasputin executing a volte as the initiation of a pirouette right, with a slightly giving outside hand. The rider should be looking over the horse's left ear. This would push the left shoulder back a little.
Right: *Eddo Hoekstra on Rasputin showing shoulder-fore on the long side. Rider demonstrates excellent seat and aids. Both photos by Roel Hoekstra.*

At the end of the first year the horse could be showing Training Level and easy First Level tests. In his first show, all that should be expected is for the horse to get used to the show atmosphere. We must try our best to avoid any bad experience (including punishing the horse for his nervousness), which the horse will remember and carry forward to future shows.

Year 2

In the second year, one can start with smaller circles, turn on the haunches, and introduction to the walk pirouette through a volte, then continue with leg yielding in the walk and trot, as a preparation for lateral work, on a 20 m circle in shoulder-fore as well as on the long side. Travers and renvers should be ridden on the second track to make it easier for the horse. The horse should be well bent on a 10 m circle, in

Dr. Hilary M. Clayton in a correct turn around the haunches in walk, with a very light contact and a rider nicely following the movement. Photo by Bob Tarr.

preparation for shoulder-in. We need the bending from the 6 m circle for travers as well as for the half-pass in trot or canter. Ride a lot of straight lines on the quarter and center line with or without halts at any spot, so that the horse learns not to rely on the kick board.

Now is also the time to initiate the canter departure from trot and walk, as well as counter canter on the long side. Mistakes to be avoided when starting counter canter are riding too deep into the corner and bending the neck too much. The counter canter should always be ridden like a normal canter.

Lisette Milner showing Eminence in Travers left in trot. Photo by Teri Miller.

Gary Lawrence on First Class showing Travers right in canter. Photo by Kathryn Affleck.

Shoulder-in by Lisette Milner on De Luxe, owned by Tina Beaman, in correct bend and flexion, with uninhibited Schwung. Photo by Susan J. Stickle.

Ride 10 m circles from A or C between the two quarter lines and change from one circle into the other at the center line in walk, trot and canter with simple changes. All circles must be ridden as identical shapes, where every step and every stride is ridden as a turn.

When the school figures are not ridden with geometric accuracy the training benefit is lost, because the horse is allowed to avoid the difficulty by falling out of balance and drifting in or out. In the simple changes it is very important to maintain a walk that is one hundred percent correct. If the walk is tense, keep the horse on the same circle until the he quiets down.

10m circles around the center line in walk, trot or canter, the latter including simple changes at crossover points. Drawing by Prof. Paul Schopf.

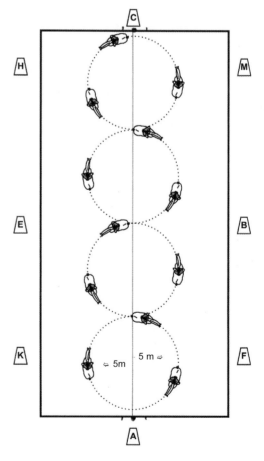

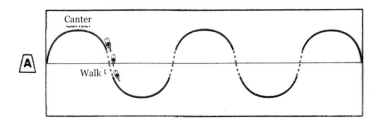

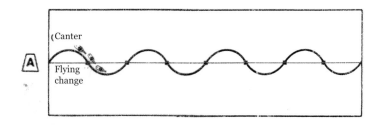

Serpentine over the centerline with simple change, which helps in setting up the flying changes. Drawings by Kathryn Rustad.

This figure eight exercise is a big help to obtain a good balance, flexion and bending. It is also a good preparation for flying changes.

With this exercise, every change from one circle to the other has to go in three phases. In the first phase, the horse is still bent on the old circle; in the second phase the horse is straight; in the third phase the horse is flexed and bent on the new circle. As the horse move to the new bend and direction, the new inside driving leg immediately engages the new inside hind leg, so the horse does not stiffen and lose his rhythm and tempo.

The same applies when riding the serpentine over the centerline with simple changes through the walk. It is important to keep the serpentines flat in order to avoid an excessively abrupt change in bend and flexion during the changes. In the next drawing you can see a very shallow serpentine over the centerline.

By this stage, the horse should accept the half halts readily because of the trust he developed during the first year of long and low riding. Through the increased engagement of the hind leg, produced by half halts, the horse will step more under the center of gravity, will become relatively more upright, and will look proud. With shoulder-fore, light flexions, short exercises in collection, medium and extended trot only for as long as the rider can maintain control and keep the horse under his seat at all times, the horse's strength is developed. In bringing the horse back from extensions, the hind leg has to be kept lively. This is the foundation for the passage and piaffe. You can also do some steps of rein back —without forcing. The horse must step back with an active and lifting hind leg and must not drag his feet. At the end of this year the horse can occasionally be ridden with a double bridle, provided that most of the work is still done in the snaffle.

At the end of this year the horse should be able to show Second Level and easy Third Level tests.

Year 3

In the third year, we should do lots of walk-canter departures, transitions between right and left canter, then counter-canter. When this is sure, we can start with flying changes, which we have to build up again through easy exercises, such as serpentines through the centerline. These shallow serpentines allow us to avoid having to flex and bend the horse too much. Under no circumstances should the aids be rough or surprising for the horse. As soon as the horse becomes frightened, the flying changes must be stopped immediately and be replaced by some simple changes.

Top: *The horse's right canter is clearly visible. His whole weight rests on the left hind leg, which is the beginning of the next stride and the first phase of the canter movement.*
Middle: *We can clearly see the second phase of the canter, with the weight on the right hind leg, as well as on the left front leg. Lastly, the right (inner) front leg lands and absorbs the whole weight, thereby creating a "floating" moment. The aids for flying changes must be given as soon as this leg lands in order for the change to occur during the "floating" phase.*
Bottom: *The flying change has already taken place during the "floating" phase. The horse lands on his right hind leg, thus initiating the first phase of the new left lead canter. Rider: Amanda Johnson on Glissade.*
Photos by Deborah Ockenfels.

Ride canter half-pass on the circle, the forehand always leading, then decrease the circles to begin training pirouettes. Do everything on both hands. In the second half of this year, series of flying changes can be made without counting the tempi. The half-pass zig-zag can begin, always riding the horse exactly straight between each flying change and the new half-pass. When riders execute the half-passes too quickly, without straightening the horse, the horse gets frightened because he feels thrown off his balance.

Trot short turns on the haunches, but always good forward in rhythm, and not too small. Think about the volte. Trot half pass in zig-zag, but always straight in the transitions between directions. Ride collected trot into short steps. Ride walk, short-step trot, out of this medium and extended trot and back to collection without the horse getting tense and going out of the short step into a kind of passage step. The horse should be able to show clearly the difference between collected trot and passage. I would like to warn everyone not to start the passage out of the medium or extended trot. The horse gets mixed-up. Do this 10 times and the horse will never come back from extended to collected trot, but will produce passage instead. The passage should only be developed through short-steps.

Never ask for the piaffe on the spot too soon. The horse should always be in a good forward movement, maintaining a good *Schwung*. Do lots of transitions in short steps, then out of this into a couple of steps forward and back to the short steps. In this way, the horse will find the balance, which allows him to execute a longer piaffe and passage. Don't practice this for too long, though, because the horse will get tired and tight, and will start to refuse and fight. These transitions can also be improved by riding careful transitions between collected, medium and extended walk without hand, just with the seat, the legs and half halts. Piaffe in hand is another possibility to teach a horse this exercise.

Half steps leading up to piaffe and passage. The author on Eva-Maria Pracht's horse.

Only a very sensitive rider like those trained by Reitmeister Egon von Neindorff, should attempt initiating the piaffe in hand.

This, however, requires the sensitivity and experience of a true master. Reitmeister Egon von Neindorff was one of those great masters. He was able to make horses dance in hand. When doing so, any haste and harshness must be avoided. "Slowly but surely" should be the motto. Once the horse shows a good piaffe in hand, without the rider's weight, and is then introduced to the rider's weight later on, this is a new and important change for the horse. He must now learn to react to the rider's weight and leg aids, instead of being touched by the dressage whip alone. The rider's dressage whip must remain an additional support, which the horse respects but does not fear.

Work on the *Schaukel* can now begin. This is a movement, sometimes required in the upper level tests, which requires the horse to take repeated steps in rein back, separated by steps forward, without loss of rhythm. When the horse is very confirmed and confident in the *Schaukel*, it is a sign that he responds very easily and precisely to the forward as well as the backward aids. The horse can only react this precisely when the rider knows exactly which hind leg is stepping, and gives the aid at the right moment. The rider uses the momentum from the backward *Schwung* of the hind leg to move forward with equal *Schwung* of the same leg.

At the end of this year the horse should go Fourth Level and Prix St. George.

Year 4

In the fourth year we take what the horse has learned in the third year and solidify it. During this year, we continue with zig-zag half-passes in trot and canter, but now with ever shorter straight sections in between. The tempi changes must now be

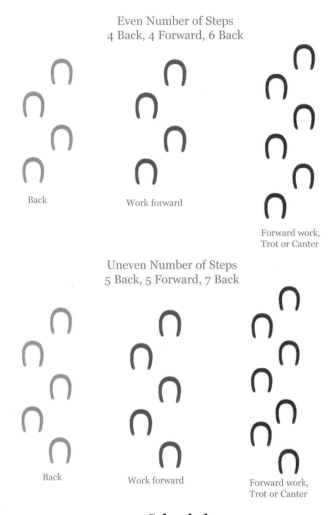

Even Number of Steps
4 Back, 4 Forward, 6 Back

Back   Work forward

Forward work,
Trot or Canter

Uneven Number of Steps
5 Back, 5 Forward, 7 Back

Back   Work forward   Forward work,
Trot or Canter

Schaukel

more precise. The one-tempi changes should be started first as three one-tempi, then-straight, then again three one-tempi again, and so on. Then the distance of straightness without flying changes between the one-tempi can be reduced, until the horse does the one-tempi changes without any tightness. If the horse gets frightened, we have to take a step back. As with everything, the beginning is the hardest, especially when it comes to the one-tempi changes. Either the rider applies the aids too early or too late. If they are too early, the horse stays in the same canter; if they are too late, the horse does two or three tempi changes. Now is a good time to begin pirouettes by asking the inside hind leg to make the smallest circle, without ever losing the quality of the canter.

The piaffe can be ridden now more and more on the spot. But as soon as the horse loses the *Schwung* and the rhythm, the horse must go out right away to recover his impulsion. The piaffe should be ridden so that we can transition to a passage instantly, and immediately back to the piaffe.

When the rider is in the piaffe and would like to go into the passage, he should mentally continue the piaffe, but transition to the passage by applying a slight forward aid. The rider should not feel any change in rhythm and should maintain the same aids. To transition from the passage into the piaffe, the rider should think about shortening the steps of the passage.

Pirouette right, nicely collected, with good bend and flexion and the rider in a good and relaxed seat. Rider: Courtney King on Idocus. Photo by Bob Tarr.

It is important that the horse maintain the same rhythm. As soon as the rider feels that the horse is losing the rhythm and *Schwung*, he must continue on in the passage, and find another place to try the transition back to the piaffe. The horse must never lose the rhythm. The horse must glide smoothly from one movement into the other.

When the horse has been trained to do correct trot-walk-trot or trot to short step transitions, he will not have too much trouble with the piaffe-passage-piaffe transitions. That is why I always stress that "cheating with the basics does not pay."

In the piaffe-passage-piaffe transitions, the rider should have always the feeling that he is riding "up to heaven." The horse should look

A magnificent piaffe, one we see from horses in nature, without being disturbed by a rider's weight or interfering aids. Photo by Paula Chmura.

very proud, the poll should be always the highest point through the relative elevation, and the nose should be slightly in front of the vertical. Every transition should be obtained with very discreet aids. The fewer aids visible to the spectator, the easier and more accurately the horse will respond. Everything should look easy and relaxed.

Lisette Milner demonstrating a very good piaffe on De Luxe, owned by Tina Beaman. Photo by Susan J. Stickle.

The same horse and rider in a passage. The rider's excellent seat and influence are proof of the relaxation of the horse.

Finally, even at this level the clear, four beat rhythm in the walk, the rider's correct seat and the correct tempo in all gaits must be preserved.

At the end of the fourth year the horse should go Intermediare and Grand Prix.

Year 5

The fifth year is the time to expect a polished performance in a Grand Prix test. If the horse becomes frightened because too many of the movements come one right after another, then we have to step back and try again a week or two later. Remember that everything takes its own time. However, don't practice the tests over and over again! Only ride pieces of the test, so you don't turn your horse into a circus horse who performs by memory instead of responding to the rider.

If we took enough time in the building of the basics, in accordance with the training pyramid, and if we never rode the horse over his limits, the horse will not have much difficulty in mastering this. Rider and horse will convey an excellent impression for the judge and the spectators through an effortless test, in which all aids remain almost invisible.

One can only achieve this according to schedule if horse, rider and trainer are working together in perfect harmony, never exceeded the horse's limit, and when rider and horse are in a harmonious partnership which is built on mutual respect and trust. The horse should be able to show Grand Prix just as well in the snaffle as in the double bridle. Every new exercise should be trained in the snaffle.

A Grand Prix horse should be trained so that any weak rider can ride him also. He should also be able to show a correct test at the lower levels. At all levels one

Jane Casnellie and Theresa Doherty hacking.

should never forget to make the work varied, interesting and fun by alternating with some hacks through the country side, free jumping, and small jumps under the rider. Everything so the horse does not get bored and sour. One should never turn a horse into a dressage or a jumping machine. Dressage horses should jump, jumpers should work their dressage, and all horses should be hacked out.

5.7 Ethics

Continuing education

The more I know, the more I know what I don't know.

Wolfgang von Goethe

How true this is especially in riding. The trainer's goal is to be successful with every horse. Each horse is different (like every person) and has to be treated as an individual. Only then will the trainer be successful with all horses. Trainers may like to think that they are competent professionals who have spent enough time learning how to ride and train horses. In fact, there is always more to learn, if just because there is always a new horse. Even the same horse can change from day to day. This is what makes riding so difficult, but also what it makes it so interesting.

If his training methods are not working, he must learn from the horse. The horse shows through his body language that he does not understand the aids. Therefore, the rider must adjust his aids so that the horse can understand them. The aids must be correct and be given at the right moment. They must also be slightly changed when the situation requires it.

A trainer never outgrows the need to learn more. The trainer must feel and correct little mistakes early, so that they do not develop into big problems. If he has started young horses in a careful and harmonious manner, the corrections are seldom big. But the trainer who has to ride many older horses that need correction will often find his own position and technique compromised.

The late Master Josef Neckermann, a world champion and Olympic gold medalist, never rode his horses without someone standing on the sideline, whether it was his wife, his trainer or his groom, who could immediately inform him of the slightest mistake. He always said that the slightest mistake can be seen much better from the sideline than it can be felt and immediately corrected from the saddle. He used to say "I try to make as few mistakes as possible, and I want somebody to correct me immediately, so that I don't make more mistakes."

Do not mask bad training by frequent re-purchases

The trainer who is always blaming the horse for the mistake and says that the horse is not good enough for the higher levels should be a red flag warning to the owner/rider. Most horses are talented, and are successful at the beginning of their training. Because of this initial success, they may start to be ridden over their limit. Unfortunately, it is often the most gifted and generous young horses who get pushed too far too fast. They become overstressed and develop chronic soreness. The horse uses the language of his resistance to remind the rider that he is asking too much of him, both mentally and physically. The bad trainer will believe that this is only stubbornness, and that rougher aids will do the trick. He uses too much spurs and whip. A horse with a strong character will try to run away, buck or rear. This leads to fighting and an ugly scene, where the rider always ends up the loser, and the sensitive spectator will get a shock from dressage. The horse becomes more and more resistant and eventually is sold off. Thus, the horse goes downhill, in spite of his promising beginnings. This way the dressage world loses very good horses and sponsors.

The horse who is kind and dumb enough, who does not resist excessive aids and unnecessary punishment, tries to comply and becomes like a slave. Everything looks mechanical; the good gaits get lost; the horse is stiff and lacks brilliance, *Schwung*, lightness and harmony. Unfortunately, this poor horse is lackluster at home and scores poorly on the show ground. He, too, may end up being sold as untalented or unsuitable.

Good training produces easy horses

My old master always said that we should train a horse that everyone can ride, by making it obedient to the softest aids. Then even a weak rider is able to ride these horses. This will not be possible if the horse is trained with excessively hard hand and leg aids, where the leg drives the horse so much that strong holding with the hand is constantly required. Those horses can only continue to be ridden by a strong rider. Some trainers are strong enough and experienced enough that they can hold a horse together and push it through a performance. Over time, however, all gaits become hard and stiff. The horse opens up his mouth to avoid the pain and pressure, puts the tongue high, takes it over the bit or lets it hang out. The horse goes behind the vertical and avoids the aids of the rider. This kind of riding is torture. Many newcomers and interested people do not feel comfortable with this and end up getting lost to this beautiful sport.

Every trainer feels pressure to show that the horse goes very well for him. But it is much more important that the owner can ride the horse easily. This can be obtained by patiently training the horse to respond to very light aids. The three gaits become more light and effortless and the whole experience becomes more enjoyable for horse and rider alike. Even the most difficult exercises can be performed without the horse getting physically and mentally over worked. Such a picture of harmony between two so completely different creatures would be a good example for everyone, especially for our young riders, and is a very good advertisement for the dressage sport. It should be the goal of every professional rider to ride his horses in a manner that everybody would like to be the owner of such a horse.

The most important duty of the trainer must always be to produce a horse that the owner can ride. The amateur owner pays for the training of his horse and has to make sacrifices for this. It is not right when a trainer believes that he should make the horses so that only he can ride them, always having good horses for shows and at home, with the owner paying for it. This is anything but a correct attitude for a trainer.

Know what you are doing—don't just imitate

I have to warn all riders and trainers against copying something that they have seen in a clinic from a very famous trainer before they have had a chance to study and practice the technique for an extended time under that trainer's watchful eye. One example is attempting to obtain a better piaffe and passage from the horse by touching the horse's front leg with a bamboo stick in the moment when he pushes away from the ground, and using a long whip in the other hand to touch the opposite hind leg in the moment when it pushes away to stimulate the hind leg to more elevation. To do this correctly you need the experience of an excellent Master. Another mistake is attempting to make the passage better with the help of the Spanish Walk. In the Spanish Walk the horse has to throw his front legs very high and the hind legs are not able to step under his body, because they can only take very short steps in order to keep himself in balance. The walk gets more and more lost.

I have also seen too many inexperienced riders and trainers try to copy the new style of training (*Rollkur*). In this method, one pulls the horse extremely deep, the chin almost touches the chest, and the head gets pulled very strong to the left and right to make the horse supple. When you observe this in the warm-up ring, you can only say that it is torture. Only very few horses will tolerate this type of riding. All other horses will turn into fighters and get sold because they are not suitable to take this type of riding.

Only a very few, highly skilled, riders can train their horses this way and get away with it. Even when those riders are very successful, it does not mean that this type of riding is the right way.

I just want to say how dangerous it is to blindly copy the training methods of successful riders and trainers without a clear understanding of how and why they work, when they are being applied correctly, and when they are being overdone. From a clinic one should only take home what one can do by oneself with your horse without hurting him physically or mentally. Dressage should be a harmonic partnership that is built on trust and respect.

Do not rush the training to impress the client

The owner should not be impressed by an overly rapid progression in the training of his horse. Most of the time this leads to slow-downs in the long run. Every horse, each one in different degrees, needs time to understand the aids of the rider. Rushing this process will cause a weak foundation, and sooner or later what is built up will collapse.

It is a great danger when a new trainer is not too sure of himself and trains a horse with whom he was entrusted to a quick success, just to impress the owner. This cannot work. He forgets that the horse must first get used to him and his aids. Even if he rides in almost the same way as the rider or trainer before him, his seat and aids will still be slightly different. The horse can certainly feel and sense this. Consequently, it is very important to take time to develop a trusting relationship between a new rider and the horse. This is most important for both a young and an experienced and well-trained horse. If the rider tries to force his style on the horse, this will be the beginning of the end of their relationship. It is important to make clear to the owner that both horse and rider need enough time to get to know each other in order to achieve a successful training.

I cannot warn often enough of the dangers of training horses too fast. This will not be good for the horse, the rider, the owner, nor for dressage riding in general. Naturally, we must have a goal, yet we must be flexible and, if necessary, be willing to go one step back.

The same is true of clinics. A good clinician will only teach the rider and the horse what they safely can do by themselves after they have returned home. If a clinician is not sure of himself, he may try a quick fix and demand exercises which are too much for rider and horse, but that make a big impression. Most of the time they will go over the horse's limit, thus creating fear. If the rider pursues the same method at home, this will invariably lead to a disaster. Weeks or months may be necessary to let the horse forget the bad experience. A horse can be ruined in the shortest of times, but one needs a very long time to regain his confidence in the rider. Even a very good rider may need months, perhaps a whole year, to recover from a bad experience, and the horse may never forget it.

Punishment

Where force is used, force shall be awakened.

Karl Jaspers

Punishment is counterproductive. For example, when the horse does not understand the aids and makes a mistake in the one tempo changes, and his rider gets angry, uses too much spur and whip, and drills again and again the one tempo, the poor horse gets frightened and makes even more mistakes.

The rider must ask himself where is the root of the problem. That is where the correction must be applied. No horse will make a mistake on purpose. Most mistakes originate from the horse's misunderstanding of the aids or from finding it difficult to comply: we have asked for something for which the horse was not yet ready, physically or mentally. When the rider gives incorrect aids in the wrong moment, the horse does not understand and does something different from what the rider expected. A very good trainer will know the mistake was his fault and not the fault of the horse. He will learn from this and will give more correct aids so the horse can better understand them. A bad and impatient rider will always blame the horse for the mistake. He loses self-control and punishes the horse. Most of the time the horse cannot associate the punishment with the mistake. The horse will end up getting increasingly frightened and tense, which will lead to more mistakes, which in turn will lead to more punishment. The horse will always connect the punishment with the immediate situation, and will remember the punishment in a similar situation. I once saw a rider finish a test with a nice straight halt, and then leave the arena with a very good walk on a loose rein. She then proceeded to beat the horse in a place where no one could see it. When I asked her why she did this, she said that the young horse had acted up in the ring, so she was punishing him. I pointed out that if the horse had made some mistakes, he had long since forgotten them, and would think that the punishment was for making such a nice halt or for a nice free walk on a long rein!

Under no circumstances should the whip or spur be used in a rage by an out of control rider. Horses that are subjected to this out of control, and to them incomprehensible, punishment will show whip and spur marks, and will start to sweat. Back in the stall the horse can get a secondary, cold, sweat. This could lead to colic because of tightness, stress and fear. With such mishandling many good horses get lost to the sport, who could otherwise be on the top. This should never happen in our training. The rider must always stay above the situation, which requires long experience, self-control, and a fundamentally decent temperament.

It may help to inform our thinking on this issue to consider whether a horse is in fact at all capable of "making a mistake." In common parlance, a making a mistake implies an intent to do an act, if not necessarily a wrong act. That intent justifies assigning blame. But horses can only "re-act"—to pain or the absence of pain, fear or the absence of fear. They have only the most rudimentary ability to formulate an intent. Moreover, horses are not born equipped to carry a rider. Therefore we can

This is the effect of good lower back and leg aids. Illustration by Sandy Rabinowitz.

hardly justify assigning blame when the horse reacts to being pressed into service to carry a rider.

Horses are not dogs. They cannot learn or retain that a behavior is "right" or "wrong." Thus, the use of the whip or spur cannot teach the horse not to do again what it did a stride or two ago. These aids can only influence the next stride, and should only be used coolly and calmly with that intent. Horses learn by repetition (i.e., what should be from what is). Use of the whip or spur after a disobedience or mistake, in a way that helps ensure that the next strides will be good additions to the horse's experience bank, is the only way they can be truly effective aids to the training. In the training, praise should be the priority. Let the horse know when he does something good, so he has pleasant associations with the work.

Horses should never be punished for spooking and shying. Generally this behavior is a sign that the horse is not yet warmed-up and focused on the work. Under no circumstances should one try to force the horse to move closer to or past the object that he is shying away from. The horse will connect the punishment with the feared object and will only get more frightened. It is much better to gradually desensitize the horse to the feared object, by not going too close to it at first. Part of the purpose of the warm-up is to bring the horse's full confidence, attention and focus to the rider. Once that is achieved, the horse can gradually be led closer through light shoulder-in or leg yielding.

Notes on abuse

We should distinguish the intentional abuse of the horse from that which is committed out of ignorance. Both are unfair to such beautiful creatures as our horses.

There are sadists who are sick and make the horse sick, hurt him on purpose, and derive pleasure from this. They may, for example, isolate the horse and give very little water and food when the horse shows too much temper during the work and at horse shows, to make him obedient. They always ride their horses over the limit to bring them into submission.

Some trainers, however, do not intend or recognize what they are doing as abuse. In recent years, a technique has become popular with which horses are ridden too short and too deep with strong hands (*Rollkur*). The result of this technique is that the horse overstretches the neck and back vertebrae, as well as the poll ligament. The shoulder gets blocked and the hind legs cannot get under the horse. Ultimately, the horse loses his correct gaits and his *Schwung*. This method encourages trainers to forget that the horse's back muscles get strong only when the *Schwung* from the hind legs is allowed an unrestricted transition over the back to the withers, neck, poll, and eventually into the horse's mouth and the hand of the rider, then back again the same way to the back and the hind legs.

Horses on whom this technique is practiced will tense up, become nervous and frightened, and will sweat profusely out of fear. This induces fear of the rider and handler, which was clearly visible at the Athens Olympics in 2004. This should never happen in our training. This type of overly deep riding certainly constitutes undue punishment and even abuse

Reitmeister Günther Festerling, who is the former president of the German FN sent me a short booklet that was sent to all professionals in Germany.[4] In this booklet he exhorted riders and trainers to go back to the proper classical training of horses. After attending the *Bundes Championat* in Warendorf, I understood why Herr Festerling had to write his booklet. We are not alone in having the problem of people taking shortcuts in the training; the same happens in Germany.

The horse should never be kept in his stall all day unless he is laid up or otherwise under specific veterinary care. Some people believe that it does not hurt the horse to stay one or two days in his stall, but this is a very big mistake and is unfair to the horse. The horse will get quickly bored and can easily start with cribbing, weaving, stall walking or fighting with his neighbors. We must remember that, in freedom, the horse is usually in motion. This is also the reason why it is a bad to stop the horse's exercise and training in the winter.

If the horse must be confined, he needs extra attention. We can keep him occupied by putting the bridle on and flexing him with a light hand, first to his easy side and then to the other side, so he chews on the bit and gives in the poll and jaw. In doing so, it is important to keep the neck straight on the withers so that the horse only gives in the poll and jowl. Check to see if the crest of the neck falls to the left in the left flexion and to the right in the right flexion. Do not allow the horse to become shortened in the neck. The poll should remain the highest point at all times. Through this exercise the horse becomes more flexible to both sides. It also prevents boredom and creates a better partnership.

---

4 See Appendix C for a translation of *Reitmeister* Festerling's booklet.

Avoid the magic bullet syndrome

Some riders will search for a "magic bullet" because of a false belief that training a horse is easier than it is, and that if something is not right there is a quick mechanical fix. This may be a resort to a new type of equipment or gadget, a switch of instructor, "clinic hopping," etc. Similarly, alternative therapies such as acupuncture, chiropractic, massage, magnet therapy, etc., can be useful tools, but they can never be a substitute for correct riding and training.

There is no "magic bullet." A correct training of the horse is possible only if the rider sees the horse as an equal partner, deserving equal respect and trust. Only then will the horse grow to Grand Prix level without any mental and physical damage. This will not happen by using a lot of tricks and artificial reins to force the horse into doing something that he cannot understand.

There will always be riders who believe they have found a magic bullet that brings them quick success, but if that magic bullet means using a mechanical device or rough and aggressive aids, the effect on the poor horse will be disastrous. This wrong kind of riding does not demand that the rider learn to control himself and his own temperament, but is based solely on controlling and enslaving our horses.

Sadly, many very good and talented horses will resist this type of training and disappear altogether from the scene because only very strong and demanding riders are able to ride them. If these horses were ridden correctly, they would make it to the top.

5.8 Summary

We have spent quite a while discussing the role of the trainer in our Circle of Trust, largely because of the huge responsibility he has. The horse did not show up at our door and ask to become a Grand Prix star. Aspirations belong to the humans in our Circle, and it falls to the trainer to work the horse and develop new muscles and new talents. This must be done carefully, in good conscience and with the deepest respect for the nature of the horse. Poor training can be one of the most cruel forms of abuse. The breeder, owner—all of our Circle, but especially the horse— have put enormous trust in the trainer. It is a great burden that must be carried with skill, grace and care.

6

the instructor

Next on our Circle comes the instructor—the teacher for riders and trainers. Whether teaching beginners or coaching Olympians, the instructor is there to uphold the high standards and lead the way for the sport. An instructor must be a more thoroughly educated professional than the trainer, well versed in theory and practice, upholding the highest standards of horsemanship. Becoming a professional instructor requires advanced study and the development of professional attitudes and ethics, as well as thorough knowledge of all training techniques. The instructor is a very important member of our Circle.

6.1 Teaching People is like Training Horses

Unlike the trainer, who may largely avoid social contact by spending all his time with his horses, instructors are in the "people business." They need to know how to ride and how to train, but in addition, they need to know how to train people. A few of our training dicta apply to instructors, albeit in slightly different ways:

"Calm, forward and straight" applies to students as well as horses: Calm—students should be taught, not subjected to yelling or boot camp drills. Forward—lessons and learning should be a progression, taking the student "to the limit, but not over." Straight—the subjects should be logical and follow from a well established theory, which was derived from the practice and developed for the practice. Jumping from one popular fad to the next, which will only serve to confuse the horse and the rider.

"To the limit, but not over the limit" also applies: the instructor needs to bring the student to learn new skills, but not over-fact them with work they are unprepared for or tasks that are too difficult.

6.2 *Characteristics of a Good Instructor*

The instructor molds the horse and rider into a single unit. He should also teach his student to respect and love his horse. It is a very difficult, but very pleasant duty.

What should this type of teacher look like?

Loves the sport and horses

He should first and foremost bring lots of love toward the horses and the sport of riding. Why else would he choose a career that means hard and often heartbreaking work, with some degree of physical risk, and with often little financial reward?

Takes personal responsibility

The basic rule is "If the student hasn't learned, the teacher hasn't taught." The instructor's job is to teach, i.e., to impart knowledge and skills and thereby to induce progress and improvement, not just to critique and criticize. It is not sufficient for an instructor simply to identify and point out problems to the student. He must be able to tell the student how to fix the problems with success.

A good instructor will try to find the mistake with himself if he cannot bring the horse and rider together in harmony. He must ask himself if he brought both to their limit or whether he exceeded their limit. A bad instructor always blames horse and student, rather than himself, when something does not work out, or there is no progress over time.

The instructor must learn from the student as the trainer learns from the horse. I learn everyday from my horses and riders. They will tell me if I gave the right correction at the right moment, whether I went up to their limit or over the limit. I never blame the rider or the horse if I do not bring them together in harmony. It is my responsibility and I have to know what I can ask from them. When I have eight riders in a clinic and if only one was not able to achieve this harmony, I ask myself at the end of the day whether I went over the limit or whether I never even reached the limit. On the next day I will try to be even more careful in solving the problem.

Prevents trouble

The good instructor sees trouble before it develops, and gives the correction before it happens. This is another way that teaching riders is like training horses. The most success happens when only positive moments are experienced. This requires that the instructor knows his theory, his practicum and his horse and rider very well, so that, in planning exercises, he can be aware of the typical mistakes that are likely to occur, and can design the exercises and his approach to them so that the mistakes do not even come up. He must also have a good eye for the harmony between horse and rider, so that he can see mistakes that are about to happen and quickly change the exercise, if necessary, to avoid them. But when mistakes do arise, he should give a clear explanation of why they happened, and instruction for correction so that the next time this same mistake can be avoided. This is a very important basis of my approach. One should never push the horse beyond the limit, so that he makes a mistake, BUT, on the other hand, we must not permit the rider to hold the horse together to try to prevent the mistake. Remember, "Show the horse what we would like him to do, and let him do it." The way to prevent mistakes is to ask the horse and rider to do only what they can comfortably and confidently achieve with just a little more effort. This is the art of the master teacher, who leads his pupils forward by never allowing them to fail. Make no mistake: this truly is an art, because it requires an unerring sense of just exactly where and just exactly how far the horse's and the rider's envelope can be pushed each and every day. Pushing not enough or in the wrong place results in no progress. Pushing too much leads to failure and possibly loss of progress that has already been made.

Having said that, we must acknowledge that mistakes will happen, because we are all imperfect at this art. It is therefore important to understand and appreciate mistakes for what they are: training opportunities. They give us yet another opportunity to "show the horse what we would like to do, and let him do it."

Knows the "next mistake"

It is not very difficult for a person to audit many clinics, watch video tapes, read books, and thereby become quite familiar with all the theory of riding. One can acquire a wealth of sayings, such as "ride from the inside leg to the outside hand," or "the horse must track up," "keep him in front of your leg," and so on. The incompetent instructor can recite these dictums, and can take his students to very advanced shows, and point out "mistakes" that every rider is making. He can then gather his students up and head off to a master clinic, and his students can hear internationally famous instructors saying the same things! Does this prove our incompetent instructor is really very good? No. The real art of teaching is being able to prevent and solve the Next Mistake.

Every horse and rider makes mistakes. Beginning riders make more mistakes and make them more often, but everyone makes mistakes. A basically competent instructor can watch anyone ride and see several mistakes at once. The job of the professional teacher is to understand "which one of the ten mistakes that my student is making right now should I correct next, and how should I correct it?" When the teacher knows what mistake needs to be corrected first, then often one or two other mistakes will disappear almost by themselves. As an instructor you have to know which mistake has the most influence. That is the one you must correct.

Once dealt with, this most fundamental mistake will often level out or eliminate other mistakes. This implies a decision about which mistakes can be ignored for now, and which ones should be solved and made to disappear right away. To ignore a mistake is easy, so long as we remember that we will need to come back to it later. Making a mistake disappear comes from re-working the lesson plan. For instance, if the horse is shying at one end of an arena, simply work at the other end. Among all the sayings and collected wisdom of centuries of horsemanship, we can always find advice that will address the biggest stumbling block on the student's path. The professional instructor should have sufficiently educated himself so that he is capable of drawing on this body of wisdom. The truly gifted instructor is able to see which is the greatest stumbling block at that moment, and have the wisdom and experience to know how to deal with it, and how to adjust his corrections to the respective situation.

To learn this art, instructors should watch master clinics and see what is not (yet) taught. Instructors frequently try so hard to give their all to students that they over-teach, trying to impart all their knowledge and eradicate all the problems at once. When watching a clinic by a master, it would be well to notice which mistakes are not being fixed and which mistakes are, and then ask yourself why? It will become obvi-ous pretty soon that some of the "ignored" mistakes disappear automatically. The master knows how to go to the root of the mistake and determine where the correc-tion has to be made, and not necessarily where the mistake appears. For instance, when the horse has difficulties in lengthening the trot, one can not push the horse for-ward more over his limit. On the contrary, one must improve the collection. When a rider has difficulties in a canter pirouette, he must not be asked to perform ten pirou-ettes in a row to make them better. In fact, the exact opposite will happen, they will get worse. Horse and rider will get frightened and more tense. Most often, the reason is not in the pirouette, but in the canter that is not good, and the horse can hardly bend on a 10 or 6m circle. This is what must be corrected. Once the horse has no more difficulties with canter and bending, the pirouettes will be no longer a problem either. We have to correct the root of the mistake, not just the symptoms. And in so doing, as with everything else, it is important to lead the horse from easy exercises to the more difficult ones.

Proceed only one step at a time! It is impossible to correct all mistakes at once. This would make student and horse frightened and tense. It would only slow down the progress. The instructor must know what correction should be the priority at all times. Most of the time, other mistakes will correct themselves.

A corollary to the "next mistake principle" is the admonition that one not follow fads in teaching. A mark of a good teacher or clinician is that he teaches a different les-son to each student, adapted to each individual horse and rider, and knows where the limit is for both.

Teaches to the limit, not over the limit

The good instructor needs to be able to correct and teach only what rider and horse can understand and digest. Good instructors and trainers always meet the chal-lenge of riding and teaching "smartly"—i.e., approaching a problem from different angles, breaking it down into easier parts, rather than hammering away at what the student or horse simply cannot yet do. No amount of repetition will overcome a basic inability. Simply put, he must recognize the limit of both student and horse, and make them work to their limit, but not over the limit.

A good instructor will orchestrate the lesson so that the success of the student is virtually guaranteed. This means that he knows what the student is capable of and what is the limit of this pair, and must carefully select what is the specific goal for that lesson. Without challenging the student, nothing gets accomplished, but asking too much leads to roughness, crude aids, tensing of the horse, and so on. If, as the lesson goes on, it does not appear that progress is being made toward that goal, then the instructor needs to change the goal for that lesson. This shows that the instructor made a wrong guess about "the next mistake" and the student was not ready to learn to correct that mistake.

There is the "danger of the day after the good ride" for the teacher also. It sounds great and very nice to have a wonderful ride where everything fits together and student and horse are almost perfect in harmony. On the other hand it brings also a great danger, because the next day the teacher and student will like to get this feeling again and immediately. Very soon one will recognize that every day will bring new and different situations, which have to be solved first. Horses, riders and teachers do not feel the same every day and are not in the same good mood either. On those days the danger is that we try to force something that was very easy the day before. In this case the teacher has to be flexible and adjust to the new situation. Impatience and force will only lead to more difficulties.

The same is true with respect to the duration of a riding lesson, which typically lasts thirty minutes to one hour. However, a riding lesson can be shorter or longer, depending on the rider and the horse. If everything is fine, there is no need to add exercises, just to "fill" one hour and to kill time. One should finish the lesson and the ride when the horse is going at his best. The horse will then take home a good memory and will come in with pleasure for the ride on the next day. It is somewhat unavoidable that, in a riding lesson, the horse is kept going for too long in hard work without stretching breaks. We get into a situation where the student almost gets it, then we ask for "just once more around, oops, OK another time around. Good!, but now one more time to prove it was not just a mistake." If one gets the feeling that horse and rider get tense after a new exercise, one should stop immediately and switch to something easier. Never do something with force, which should never exist in training or teaching. In all this, it is important to remember that not all students necessarily learn the same things in the same order or at the same pace.

This is equally important when teaching a clinic. In a clinic it is very important to quickly recognize what we can ask of the rider and the horse, in order to avoid exceeding their limit. One can never expect anything from a student who does not understand, nor from a horse that is pushed beyond his limit. Riders and horses should not be frightened, as nothing can be accomplished if they are fearful. On the contrary, one must impart confidence in their own abilities. One should also observe how the student warms his horse up, so that one can help him and give him advice for a correct warm-up, so he is able to do this correctly by himself, once he has returned home. The warm-up should be part of the lesson. A good warm-up will determine the quality of the riding lesson, as well as of the test at a show.

It is wrong to ask something from horse and rider that they will never be able to do at home by themselves. The rider would get unsure and lose his patience. This, in turn, leads to harsh and unfair aids, and eventually the rider develops fear, and his horse can't handle this exercise. One should only ask so much from rider and horse, exercises that they can do easily at home, thus enabling them to progress gradually, step by step.

At the end of a good lesson, the student will have a sense of accomplishment and the feeling that he has taken a small step towards their goal, and he will look forward to his next lesson with impatience and anticipation. He should also recognize, however, that there will be a long road to near perfection, and many small and short steps will be necessary to get there. Each one of the steps must be correct. It's easy for a rider to feel that he needs to work a lot and push ahead rapidly with large steps to make progress. However, the beauty of riding is that less work but good work is always better than a lot of bad work.

I have to think back years ago when I helped Diana Rankin prepare for almost one week for the Tournament of Champions in Chicago. I let her ride most of the time basic exercises to correct better relaxation, bending, and transitions. After a couple of days she asked me if we should not work on some Grand Prix exercises. I told her that Ladykiller already knew these exercises. It was not necessary to work on those but rather just let him do them—show him and let him do it. She was very happy when she won the Grand Prix, Grand Prix Special and Musical Kur, even without too much training of Grand Prix exercises.

In life, a little but good effort is better than a lot of bad effort. This is particularly true with regard to riding. Many times one sees riders doing the exact opposite. When the rider or the instructor tries to speed up the process by taking large steps, trouble can arise. In all likelihood, this will lead to mistakes that, in the end, will take much longer to correct. These mistakes accumulate slowly, often unnoticed. A little mistake uncorrected here, another there... Riders are sometimes very skillful at coping and hiding their mistakes, but as they accumulate, a major problem is in the making. By the time the unskilled observer (or student) recognizes the error, we have gone well over the limit, and the undoing is a major job. The wake-up call always comes when it is far too late.

So-called short cuts only create a feeling of uncertainty for both horse and rider. Each rider and each horse need time to develop mutual trust. Short cuts, in reality, take much more time, because the rider has to go back again and work through the problems all over again, this time correctly. When things have to be done over again correctly, the rider can become bored and disillusioned. They thought that they knew how to do all this stuff, and now they are just learning the same thing over again. (It is ironic that the students who will take well to this re-doing are the perfectionists, who would have been comfortable with short steps in the first place!) Furthermore, we now must re-train the horse as well as the student. The horse has learned to deal with all of the student's mistakes in various ways, and going back over the same ground a second time, we will have to overcome and sometimes eliminate what the horse has now added to the mix.

Helps everyone

In Germany, there are many different riders in a club—beginners, advanced, dressage riders and jumpers. It is the duty of the teacher to give his best to each one of them. The first rider in the morning as well as the last rider in the evening all have the right to receive the teacher's best effort.

When I started at the University Riding School in Munich as head teacher, I asked only for advanced riders in my classes. But after a year, I found out that this was a mistake, and I ended up also taking on the beginners. When the students came to me as advanced riders, I had to spend a long time re-training them, and I found it easier to start them out on the correct path as beginners. What we say about horses applies equally to people: What is not done correctly at the beginning can never be re-done.

I have been asked many times why I take teaching so many weak riders in my clinics so seriously, instead of teaching only higher level riders. My answer is always: We have many more basic riders than advanced riders. The basic riders need the most help, so we bring them right away on the right track and make the riding easier for them and their horses. Most often the top riders have their own trainers and are happy with this system. Nothing is more disturbing and confusing than to go to many trainers and clinicians, just to try out their systems. "Too many chefs spoil the broth."

Many times one has to wonder why the horse does not resist more because of the mistakes and confusion the rider introduces along the way. Only his unending patience and devotion allows him to tolerate our mistakes and wrong turns, and we have to be thankful to the horse for putting up with us. But the trust between the teacher, rider and horse can be strained. One should not let things get so far. It is very hard to fix it again. Complete and utter trust must exist between horse, rider and instructor. Only then can we expect to be successful. This was also the reason why I gave my four videos the title "A Matter of Trust."

The well being of our horses and riders should be sacred, and we have to do everything not to get them in any danger. To fulfill your responsibility to them, you must take both each day to their limit but not over their limit. This was always my teacher's priority and it has become mine as well.

Is encouraging and praising

Praise will often lead back to the correct way.

Leo Lohberger

The good instructor encourages his student with a lot of praise when he does something right and not just discourages him with too many corrections. This is especially true in sport of riding, where so many things have to fit together for even the best horses and riders to have success. The teacher has to encourage his students all the time and not only correct mistakes. He must also praise immediately, if something has gone well. Every beginner and every advanced rider is making smaller and bigger progress. This positive progress is what we should build up. Even adult students have fragile egos, are often uncomfortable on the horse, and need reassurance and praise.

I am reminded of a *Bereiter* who came to me to be prepared for his *Reitlehrer* exam. When listening to his first lesson, I was very astonished that he never praised his rider. He was constantly correcting him, although the student did rather well many times. On the next day I taught him in exactly the same way as he had taught his student. I only corrected him without saying that he had some good moments. After the ride he came to me to ask if I was not satisfied with his riding, because I never praised him. I then explained that I wanted him to feel what it is like only to be corrected without receiving any praise. This was the best lesson for him, because from this moment on he changed his way of teaching so that his students could develop trust and comfort and thus advance much faster. "Praise inspires," my old master told me, and I try to apply this when I teach my students. Instructors should also teach their riders to treat their horses the same way and praise them when they do something right. The rider should not be too lazy to take the reins in one hand so he can praise the horse with the other hand.

Is patient

A good instructor has lots of patience. Teaching daily lessons can be tiring, because you will have to repeat the same things again and again. If we have to deal with students who have lots of trouble understanding, we should not give up on them. We need to be willing to use every tool we can think of: mounted demonstrations, pictures, videos and discussions. The teacher should encourage them and make clear that riding can be very difficult, but is also one of the most rewarding sports, when the rider is able to gradually achieve unity and harmony with his horse. Each student will learn something only at the precise moment when all the factors necessary to learn that things have come together. We can never truly know when that moment will arrive, so we have to accept that it will be necessary to tell the student something over and over. We must never think "I've told you that a thousand times and you've never gotten it, so I'm not going to bother to tell you that any more." The student may get it on time 1001! How many times in your own riding have you thought: "Gee, I've heard/read that so many times, but it suddenly just clicked?" Therefore, never give students the feeling that they will never learn. Most of the time, those riders love their horses and the sport. Every rider who wants to learn is equally important. The same applies to the horse. Even when we know full well that a rider should have a better horse, we have to make the best out of this. Most riders do not have the money to buy a really top class horse but still love their horses. You will find neither any human being nor any horse without mistakes, but each has value.

With all this, it is important for an instructor to avoid burnout. It is very hard on a teacher who teaches the whole day, mostly beginners. He gets tired and numb, meaning that he hardly recognizes any mistakes any longer, and corrects everything mechanically. He needs something to recover his spirit, perhaps it is a very good horse he can train and show, taking the time to build up this horse step by step. He should do this at all cost before teaching his riding lessons, when he still has enough patience for his horse.

My old master Colonel H.W. Aust, to whom I owe more than just my equestrian career. He also polished my character and developed me as a human being. He has always been my role model.

Is a role model

The good instructor will always be a role model to his students, through his knowledge, attitude and correct appearance. All students like to emulate their teacher, and want to be proud to have been taught by him. He will be respected, and neither horse and nor rider will be afraid of him. In the student you recognize his master or teacher. It is the respect for this wonderful sport, for horses and teacher.

Dress always clean, in polished boots and riding attire. This does not need to be a major effort. All riding equipment is very expensive and will last a long time if you take good care of it. Every student would like to be like his teacher.

Manners. They should be such that one is happy to be around him. He should always be helpful and polite to everyone.

Attitude. Always correct. In every situation he should be calm and supportive of the riders. Also, if he has private problems, he should get help, because every personal problem detracts from his ability to give his best effort to his students.

Is a pedagogue

A good instructor is also a pedagogue and devoted to learning and to the study of how to impart learning. An outstanding rider and successful competitor is not necessarily a good teacher. The natural rider feels mistakes almost before they happen and can make corrections immediately and instinctively. This is fine and admirable and necessary for the finest balance between horse and rider. But this does not necessarily give this rider the necessary patience and understanding of the human learning process or the appreciation of the particular sequence of experiences that a student must have in order to develop a good feel. When writing my first book, I realized that so much of what I do, I do by instinct. Now I had to truly analyze the theory to make it easier for the readers to understand. It was very hard work for a practical man like myself, but it was rewarding to acknowledge that I could make riding easier, by making the theory more accessible and understandable through the book.

Thus, the instructor must be more than a successful competitor—the instructor must study, understand, and be able to easily articulate correct theory. Study of theory is accomplished through the many excellent books on the subject, by watching videos and by attending clinics.

But in addition to a thorough knowledge of theory, effective teaching requires many years of experience to manage every situation that may come up—often several in rapid succession. What makes it even more difficult is that horses, riders and situations change constantly, and even the best corrections may have to be altered slightly to fit the situation. The effective teacher must be a quick and accurate diagnostician.

As an instructor, you can continue to develop both your understanding of theory and your diagnostic skills by attending clinics, either riding or watching, or by watching your students ride in one. I will never understand a teacher who sends his students to a clinic without coming along to watch them. I would want to know what the clinician is doing with my rider and horse. It would help my own teaching a lot. I am always saddened by the fact that very few professionals take the opportunity to watch and learn. Watching and learning from what other teachers focus on or ignore, and what exercises they use to achieve their goals can help a lot, and one should never stop learning. Often, these professionals who do not bother to watch give the impression that they already know everything, or they do not have enough interest in continuing their education. Especially in clinics, the opportunity to see so many different riders and horses, and to learn different ways to help these riders, is unparalleled. Only by watching so many horses and riders, can an instructor formulate his or her own best way to teach.

When I think back to my training time, I rode eight horses every day for eight years under my old master, in dressage and jumping, young and experienced horses, and horses that needed retraining. I also had to groom all eight horses, clean out their stalls and clean the tack every day. Even with all that to do, when I had even just a little bit of time I would run down to the arena to watch my master ride or teach, to learn as much as I could from him.

Take care, however, to take only the good stuff home and leave the bad stuff with the bad clinician!

Even more important is to realize that learning by observing clinicians should be "the icing on the cake" of a single theoretical system obtained through a long period of study under the guidance of a single, qualified teacher and master. When well grounded in a unified system, you are able to evaluate how a particular clinician's methods fit into the theoretical framework that guides you each day. One of the most common mistakes that I have seen is instructors going once to see a "big" clinician, coming home and completely changing their teaching. For example: an instructor who observes piaffe being taught with a bamboo stick in one hand to bring up the front legs further, and a long dressage whip in the other to activate the hind legs. On the way home he immediately buys some bamboo sticks, which will be used back home on his poor horses by inexperienced trainers. The fact that this method requires a great master with many years experience to achieve a truly improved piaffe and passage was completely forgotten.

The students are confused by the new revelations, but the importance of the clinician is impressed on them, so they stumble along. Unfortunately, within another few months, the instructor goes to another clinic, coming home with yet another new idea. It is important to remember the adage that your job is to teach the students what they don't know, not what you don't know! If it is something that you have just seen or tried for the first time, you don't know it! We have to teach the student only what he can understand and can work on without exceeding his own and his horse's physical and psychological limit. Trying to force fit what you just observed at a clinic to every student and every horse in your barn would violate your duty to be a good diagnostician and to identify and correct "the next mistake" of each individual horse and rider pair.

Is a diplomat

A good instructor knows not only how to handle horses, but how to handle students as well. Many books on riding theory discuss the sensitive nature of the horse, and how he must be guided with care and respect. Our human students deserve the same. It is interesting how many instructors have true empathy with horses, but completely disregard the human student.

In Germany, the riding teacher works mostly in riding clubs. He has to manage the business, teach daily lessons to beginners and advanced riders in dressage and jumping, train young, older and problem horses in the arena and outside. He has to take care of students at the shows, treating all members as fairly as possible, which is really never easy. We trained very seriously for five years for this profession, with respect to both riding and management. However, the profession also requires us to be an even better diplomat. This was something that they did not teach us. This you have to acquire by experience. I was very lucky to have such a good master who was also a great diplomat and who tried to teach us this aspect also. I will always be very thankful to him. Without him I would not be what I am today and I could not help our wonderful horses. If you chase away the people, you cannot help their horses.

Your diplomatic skills as an instructor can be tested in a number of ways.

One challenge is how to handle the student who "just doesn't get it." Sometimes you may find yourself asking: "Is it wrong just to baby-sit?" It is, in fact, a mistake to assume that a student is not capable, and "will never get it."

One needs to explain things in many different ways, so that the student can find the one way that makes sense to him. Surprisingly, he sometimes understands immediately, when one just uses a different expression or another word. Often it is very good when another rider draws some attention to our possible mistakes. For example: During a clinic in Atlanta, Georgia, a spectator/rider told me that I use the wrong expression (language difficulties), speaking of "slower," instead of "shorter." Since that time I try to remember.

Don't get angry at a student for asking questions. If a student asks questions, this is a sign that he is interested in knowing exactly what is going on. This should not lead to a theory lesson, of course. Not too many questions should be asked during the actual riding lesson. Riding can only be learned through riding. The theoretical knowledge, however, is very important also in order to understand why things happen the way they do. I know all too well how difficult it is to teach very intelligent riders because they analyze everything. The same happened with my friend Dr. Hans Hebel in Munich, who always wanted to know everything in detail. Sometimes our lessons where more question and answer sessions than riding lessons. One day I had to tell him very seriously and clearly that thinking a lot is very good, but that riding skills must be acquired mostly through practice and intuition. Of course, it is very important that we know how everything is working and why one does this and that. However, we can learn this from theory, books and videos. And yet, all this material alone does not make a good rider. He needs a horse and a teacher who can help him to put the theory into practice. Theory is created from the practice and is for the practice. Dr. Hebel did work very hard, practicing every day in the very early morning, before going to work at his pharmacy. Through this dedication and effort, he was able to bring a horse, by himself, to the Grand Prix level. Throughout this process, he would call me in Canada to ask for help about whatever training problem or question that may have arisen. I told him what I thought was the reason for the problem and what I considered the best way to resolve these difficulties. In general, in a few days he would call me back to thank me and say that "it worked."

It is extremely difficult to teach students who tend to lose their patience easily. It is often hard to "get to" these students, without their taking criticism personally and letting their frustration out on their poor horses. Another difficult case is when the rider himself has not trained a horse, but only rides already trained horses and has the feeling that he knows everything, forgetting, however, that the instructor has the experience of many years of teaching and riding maybe hundreds of horses.

But the good instructor does not make it easy for oneself by ignoring questions. We all like our students to make progress. We should be thankful that the student is thinking but he should not ask the teacher for every little thing that comes up, because this should be done in a theory lesson, rather than disturbing the mounted lesson. In German they would say "Shut up and ride."

One must insist that the rider not lose patience and does not blame the horse.

Knows when to let go

It is interesting to note how quickly students become emotionally attached to their instructors, and how unable they are to critically evaluate the service they receive. Therefore it is the duty of the instructor to realize when he has reached the limit of his own ability to help the student, and to assist the student in finding another instructor to help the student continue his progress. It is a compliment to our successful teaching when our student outgrows us!

6.3 Characteristics of a bad instructor

Arrogant, rough, boastful

A good instructor is not arrogant, nor believe that he is God and knows everything. He is not rough or boastful in his lesson, his riding —or in his daily life for that matter.

Many times, when the student makes a small mistake, the instructor will get on the horse to show the student how to ride the exercise correctly. At this point the instructor should never lack self-control, try to show-off, or use overly strong aids and punish the horse, who may simply not yet be ready for the exercise. The instructor may have thought that the horse and rider were ready for a new exercise, and may in fact have been haranguing the student about the difficulties. When he is on the horse himself, he realizes that he has made a mistake, and that the horse is not ready. This is not the time to demand that the horse learns these exercises. If the horse is not ready, then the exercise must be changed to teaching how to prepare the horse better for the movement. Lacking patience, a bad instructor will resort to whip and spurs, rough aids and force in a misguided effort to hide the fact that he did not know that the horse was not ready. He may have hidden his lack of foresight, but he has exposed his lack of patience and tolerance for all the world to see. He has to cover this up by inventing theories for why such rough training is "necessary." Now the student has "learned" why one needs to abuse horses—an affront to all horsemanship.

Impatient, sarcastic

A good instructor never loses patience with his students nor make sarcastic remarks. If a student asks the teacher when is the correct time to give the aids, and he tells him "you will feel soon enough and learn soon enough when the right moment is," then we can only conclude that the instructor is too overworked to give the student's question its proper attention, or does not know himself when the right moment is. Of course it takes a long time to learn to feel the correct timing of the aids, but until the student has learned, it is necessary to repeatedly tell the student when the proper moment is, with patience and understanding.

If the instructor is unable to give quiet and clear directions, and loses his temper and patience too quickly, then he does not have the right to teach, because the responsibility to the rider and the horse is enormous. Most of the time it is the instructor's own lack of know-how and the compassion that comes with experience that leads to frustration with the student. It is easy and understandable to watch a student struggling with the most basic skill, and think "why is he having such trouble with such an easy thing!" At those times it is best to try and think back to our own beginning days, for a quick dose of humility and compassion, and perhaps some insight into why we struggled with this very same thing, and perhaps to what instructions and exercises helped us through it.

The instructor must have the patience to keep repeating corrections as long as necessary for the student to learn. I have heard instructors say "I have told you twice, that is enough!" How soon we forget how long it took us to learn the most basic things. The instructor who cannot be bothered to repeat corrections was probably himself taught by someone who did have patience, and told him hundreds of times how to fix this or that problem. Failure to follow instructions does not necessarily mean disrespect by the student, but may originate in deeper feelings of insecurity. Bad habits become lodged in riders' feelings of "comfort" and familiarity. If we are to change these habits, we need to replace what the student perceives as comfortable. It may take many, many efforts. You should tell your students that you will be making corrections over and over because you understand how hard it is to break old habits. Letting them know that you understand their problem helps them stay focused on correcting it, rather than developing feelings of failure and incompetence.

Yelling

A good instructor does not scream or yell as this would only make horse and rider frightened, without leading to more success. My old master always reminded us that it is wrong for us to yell at a student. This only shows up our inability to fix the mistake in a calm and correct manner.

Lacking integrity and professionalism

A good instructor never makes negative comments about another instructor, rider, farm or horse, and does not allow himself to be drawn into gossip. Also, when a student goes to a show and scores badly, then the instructor should not blame the judge. Either the student was sent to the show before being fully prepared, or the instruction was incorrect.

Lacking humility

When an instructor receives advice from a more experienced teacher, he should not take offense, but should have the courage to reflect on what was said, and understand that the more experience one has, the more one wants to help. Be thankful to anyone who shows an interest in helping you, as you should always be helpful to all other instructors.

Uneducated, uninformed

An instructor who does not strive constantly to improve his knowledge, understanding and skills in this very challenging and complicated sport is a thief. He is stealing not only his student's money, but also his student's and the horse's life—both of which are too short to waste on an ignorant teacher.

6.4 *Why is it difficult to find good instructors?*

First, classical riding is still a relatively new discipline in North America. There has not been time to develop a solid base of educated and experienced riders, from which a group of qualified teachers could be developed.

However, the real reason is that we have very few trained teachers of teachers, and, until recently, no system for producing them. Most of our well-known and successful professionals got there through their riding experience, by taking clinics, by scoring well in the show-ring, or through judging. There are so few of these that they have too many horses and riders in training to take the time to teach professional instructors. Moreover, judging is not teaching, and while the skills of observation and knowledge of how a horse should go are needed by both judges and teachers, the instructor has the greater burden of needing to know not only what is wrong and what is right, but how to get from wrong to right, and how to get the student from wrong to right.

In short, there are very few facilities where professional riders can train under skilled teachers, on confirmed schoolmasters, within a coherent and correct theoretical system.

The huge North American land mass makes it almost impossible to establish a centralized, or at least correct, system of producing trained teachers. Although a beginning has been made toward a centralized system, it will still take many years before its influence will be widespread.[5] This was the reason why I wrote my book and also made the videos, in order to help those riders and teachers who are far away and have to work their horses most of the time by themselves.

The hope is that we can institute a centralized professional instructor program in North America with standards and facilities similar to those in Germany and other European countries. It is easy to hope for such a situation. It is more sobering to consider the difficulties that will arise. In Germany the centralized system that is so successful was developed by the military over centuries, when the Cavalry was the most important unit of the army. The will and authority of the Chiefs of Staff could create and maintain such an institution, and did not need the agreement of a wide number of regional horse organizations.

Even if a centralized facility like the *Deutsche Reitschule Warendorf* were established, travel to and residence at such a centralized facility would be a much bigger burden in North America than in Germany, since the size of Germany is little bigger than Texas. We could try to envision regional centers, but can you imagine such centers, (with federal government support), in every region of the country? Where should we get all the necessary trainers? Which path can we take?

The task would not be easy. It took a lot of idealism and the willingness to take financial risks, for Hans Pracht and his wife Eva-Maria to build an equestrian training center in Cedar Valley, Ontario, (IESS—International Equestrian Sport Service) in the early 1980's, to give riders in North America the opportunity to learn on good schooling horses. Everything I have said above argued against its long term success, and sadly proved correct. This was even more true for the more recent idea to build something like this in Warendorf, to give riders from North America the possibility to train with German teachers on good horse material, in great indoor and outdoor arenas, where they would also have the possibility to take their exam as *Bereiter*. But it

---

5 The USDF and USEA Instructor Certification Programs are making attempts at this.

proved to be too difficult and too expensive to bring riders from overseas to Germany. I really wished for this project in Warendorf to be successful, but I already had doubts from the beginning, because I saw what happened to I.E.S.S. Unfortunately, my doubts became true. Today it is just a riding school like so many others in Germany.

While we do not have a centralized system of instructor education and efforts at certification and examination are just being started, the standards of quality, skill and professional ethics of the professional instructor must be upheld. It is amazing how many people pay good money and give years of their lives to "learn" riding from a successful teenager. At the university, everyone knows that it is much better to be taught by a full professor than by a graduate student or teaching assistant. Winning a few shows, and riding at a higher level than one's students does not qualify a person to teach. Although this may be done quite frequently, it does not mean that this practice is either good or ethical.

One problem with learning how to ride is that it can quickly go from casual pastime to a lifetime passion. Having a local friend help you have fun is one thing, but if the inexperienced teacher lacks an appreciation for safety, "fun" can quickly turn into disaster. Furthermore, a lack of knowledge and training can quickly send the student off on a wrong track that will waste precious time and money, and likely cause undue suffering to the horse.

Summary

We often hear talk about how difficult riding is because the horse and rider have to come into harmony, with two beings joined as one in a dance of grace and power. This is undoubtedly true, and I have said it in this book. But if that is true, then teaching riding must be even more difficult, because you have to bring three beings into one—the instructor must communicate and establish rapport with the student and thereby with the horse.

7

the groom

The professional groom, for the horse who is lucky enough to have one, is second only to the owner in his importance to the horse's happiness and welfare. The groom is the horse's advocate, protector, nurse, and mother, and must know every inch of the horse's body, mind and soul. The services performed by a great groom makes him one of the most important members of our Circle, but it is a role that often goes unrecognized, under-appreciated and sometimes, unfortunately, unperformed.

Let me take a few words to describe a vanishing species: the classic groom of years gone by. He would be among the first in the barn in the morning, and the last to go home at night, sometimes in just a small room to call his own. These rooms would often be located in or near the barn, so the groom could see when the horse was sick, or if something happened to the horse and it needed his help. Often these grooms were underpaid and their work did not get the appreciation it deserved. The groom's role was to stay on the sidelines and in the background. But he was the person whom the horse knew best, as he spent more time with him than anyone. The rider might be with the horse only a few hours a week. All the rest of the time it was the groom who was with the horse. Often, the horse would become more attached to the groom than to the rider. He would feed and water the horse, clean him as well as his stall, bring him to the turn out paddock and then back again to the barn, put the blanket on and take it off when necessary. If it was too hot, he would cool him off by washing him, or by trying to get a draft through the stable, or by watering the aisle to cool it off.

He would also be always on hand when the rider needed his help. On the show grounds, the groom would check the stall to make sure there were no sharp objects that could hurt the horse during the night, and then take care to provide the horse with bedding, food and water. Often, the groom would sleep in one corner on a straw bed, from where he could watch out for his horse. He would rise early enough to make sure the horse was fed, watered, braided and sparkling clean when the rider showed up in the morning, and well before the time when the horse would be put to work. He would then make sure that the horse would return to a clean stall and fresh water and hay after the ride.

His job would also be to bring the rider and his horse to the warm-up ring, bringing along a sponge and rag ready to clean the horse and the rider's boots once more, and take off the horse's leg wraps before they went in the ring. He would also hold the rider's coat, show program, fly spray and anything else that might be needed. The classic groom of yesteryear took great pride in his horse's and his rider's appearance and performance. During the competition he would cross his fingers, sometimes pressing them so hard that they hurt. If both did well, he was very proud, taking the horse away from the tired rider and leading him back to the barn, where he would groom the horse and take care of the tack. While the rider might be already celebrating with his friends, the groom mostly celebrated with his horse by himself, and was proud and happy with him and the success. If the competition did not go as well as expected, he was sad for his horse and rider, comforting him, and saying the next time for sure it would be better.

At the end of the show he would clean out the stable, load the horse and bring him back home. At home the trailer had to be cleaned and the horse taken care of. After watering and feeding one more time, the groom finally retired, very tired but happy with his horse, arising the next day to resume the familiar routine of his care. A monument should be built to honor these classic grooms for their devotion to their horses. It is a pity very few of those fine people are still around. If you still have one of those loyal ones, you cannot be thankful enough. If you don't, the role of "the classic groom of yesteryear" must be played by you!

The hallmark of the classic groom is that he always puts the welfare of the horse above his own comfort. This means first and foremost that he ensures that the horse's physical needs are met. But the groom also has a highly important role in the horse's emotional and psychological well being, and a key component of that role is the act of grooming itself.

Horses groom each other in the herd and this act of grooming helps establish herd bond between horses. The daily grooming ritual similarly helps cement our bond with our horses. If the same grooming ritual is followed each day—even down to always picking the horse's feet in the same order, for example—it really reinforces the horse's sense of security. Later in this chapter I have set out in detail the grooming ritual I always followed with my horses.

Tacking and preparing to ride need to be done with the same calm and careful approach. It makes no sense to rush and tack up as quickly as possible. This will not make the horse relax before being worked. To bring the horse in harmony with the rider, start when on the ground to establish a trusting communication between horse and rider.

The saddle must fit properly. It is beyond the scope of this book to discuss the details of saddle fitting, as this was already mentioned in my first book and in my videos. But one should always get expert advice to make sure the saddle properly

A good tack room, as it should look, with bridles and saddles neatly arranged. This is Candlewood Farm, owned by Neil Schwartzberg. Photos by Jane Casnellie.

fits the horse. One should never forget that the mouth and back of the horse are the most sensitive parts. How can a horse bring high performance when he is suffering pain and soreness in these parts? It is particularly important to leave enough room over the withers and through the spinal channel, because pressure in these areas can lead to acute pain. Many nerves go through the withers. The saddle should be re-fitted every year, because an incorrect and unbalanced seat of the rider will make one side of the saddle "sink" to one side, thereby exacerbating the effect of the incorrect seat. Almost every rider has one leg longer than the other. This must be corrected by compensating with the appropriate length of the stirrups. Note also, that the horse's back may change over time and with training, necessitating additional saddle fittings. The saddle pads should always be clean to ensure that dirt is not pressed into the skin on the horse's back.

A correctly fitting bridle is equally important. If the bit is too high, it will pull too much in the horse's mouth; if too low, it will allow the horse to play with it or to put the tongue over or above the bit, or let it hang out. If the brow band is too short, it will exert excessive pressure on the head and ears; if too long, it will flap up and down on his head. Many riders make the mistake of making nose band very tight, thinking that this will help put the horse on the bit, or at least prevent him from opening his mouth to evade the bit. This has absolutely the opposite effect! An overly tight noseband can make it difficult for the horse to breathe. This could cause the horse to get frightened. Many horses will refuse to go forward completely, but get over it immediately if the noseband is loosened. Even if the horse does not react so dramatically, his performance will still be affected. Straining to open his mouth against an overly tight noseband will make him stiff in the jaw. Moreover, his attention will be entirely focused on the discomfort he feels, and he will be unable to put his relaxed attention where it belongs: on his rider.

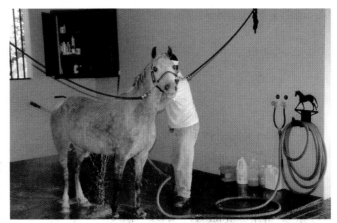

Two SwanS Farm, owned by Carol Cohen, here with the groom John. Photo by Mark Neihart.

For your safety and for the comfort of the horse, saddle and bridle should be cleaned and inspected after every use and lightly conditioned frequently. When the leather is still warm from use it is easy to clean and condition.

The way in which you care for and store your grooming equipment and your tack signals to the world how high are your standards of care. Visitors are justified in assuming that a tack storage and grooming area where everything has its own labeled place, that can be easily found even in the dark, and where no unnecessary objects are left lying around, means that the horses, also, are given the best and most attentive care. It goes without saying that a disorganized and dirty area justifies the opposite assumption.

My grooming regimen

Whenever handling or working around the horse, it is important to act calmly and soothingly toward the horse. We should take time and not hurry, and always use the same routine every day. Here is the routine that I always used.

Before leading the horse out to the grooming place, I would first clean out his hooves. This would help to keep the aisle clean and ascertain that the hooves were clear of nails or stones. I would make sure that the grooming place was not drafty. Horses are much more sensitive to draft than to cold.

Very clean grooming tools, which must be cleaned after each use.

Left: *An unattractive "pheasant tail."* Right: *This is how a nicely groomed tail should look. Photos by: Joan Adler*

I would start the cleaning of the horse on the head, very carefully, so that the horse did not get frightened, using a soft brush or mitt. A curry comb should never be used on the head, hip bones or on the legs, as it can hurt the horse.

After this I started with the curry comb on the left side on the neck, because one does everything first from the left, like putting the bridle and saddle on, lifting up the feet for cleaning, etc. Again, it is very important to follow the same routine every time, because the horse equates sameness and routine with security. After currying, I continued by going over the same areas with the body brush, very carefully, over the horse's whole body, against and with the direction of the hair growth, taking care not to brush too hard over the bony parts. After every three or four strokes, I cleaned the brush with the curry comb. I knocked the dust out of the curry comb often, by tapping it against the stone floor. My old master made sure we were doing the job right by counting the dust marks of the curry combs where we tapped them! After finishing with both sides, I cleaned the horse with a lightly damp rag from the head to the back, starting again on the left hand side on the head. I learned to fold this towel so I could always work with a clean spot and to avoid the end of the rag flying around and scaring the horse. By folding and refolding it I could always keep a clean side out. I washed the towels several times per week.

While the horse was out of the stall, I took this time to quickly take out the manure, level and bank the bedding, and add more bedding if necessary.

Finally, I cleaned eyes and nose with a soft sponge, as well as the inside of the ear, where a lot of dust can gather.

I always took care that the areas under the tail, and the genitals of mares, stallions and geldings were kept very clean to avoid any itching. These parts I cleaned

An ideal wash stall, fitted with rubber mats, heat lamps and a ventilator. Candlewood Farm, owned by Neil Schwartzberg. Photo by Jane Casnellie.

with a soft, wet sponge at least four or five times a week. I washed the tail often, but only brushed the top, not the bottom, to avoid losing too much hair and making the tail very thin (pheasant tail). Instead of brushing, before going to work I would pick the horse's tail free of straw, shavings or debris. Before putting my grooming tools away, I cleaned them, so that they were always clean when I needed them on the next day.

When clipping the horse with electric clippers, I was careful that the horse did not step on the wires (or any other wires that might be lying around the barn) to prevent electric shock. Shod horses are particularly susceptible to cutting through the insulation around electric cables. How often we clipped depended on the horse, whether he sweated a lot and/or had a very long winter coat. We always clipped our horses after October 10th. One clipping was usually enough to last until the horse changed his winter coat. However, the coat of warm bloods sometimes grew faster than that of Thoroughbreds and needed to be clipped more often. After clipping we blanketed the horses immediately, so that they did not catch a cold. After a new clipping we also put a quarter blanket on the horse at the beginning of the training, securely fastened so that it did not fall off.

When the grooming was done, I always cleaned the grooming place or wash stall right away, picking up manure and hair, and leaving it ready for the next horse and rider.

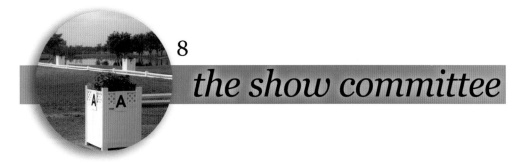

8

the show committee

Many horses lead long and happy lives without ever seeing the inside of a show grounds. However, for those horses for which a show career is on the agenda, many of the members of our Circle of Trust must come together to work even more closely and effectively.

8.1 Classical vs. Competitive Dressage

First, since my major training focus in recent years has been in the sport of dressage, I feel compelled to say a few words about the controversy surrounding the issue of whether there are two types of dressage: "classical" and "competitive." In my view it is a mistake to say that "classical dressage is a different training matter than 'competitive dressage'."

It becomes different only when the trainer tries to get quick success by using short cuts. Those who believe that they can only get the horse to the top with rough aids and force are the sources of this thinking that there is a big difference between classical training and show riding. When I hear this, I can only shake my head in disbelief. From out of this thinking a completely different training method has been created, resulting in horses being ridden every day over their mental and physical limits and too much force being used.

Young horses must be built up slowly but surely through the training pyramid: rhythm, tempo, relaxation, balance, contact, "Schwung," straightness and collection. These are the prerequisites for the correct gymnastic development of the horse. When the pressures of the competition schedule cause artificial training deadlines to be imposed, the relaxation, balance and Schwung are the first to go. Lacking regard for the most sensitive part of the horse, his mouth, strong hand aids are applied to put him on the bit right away. The horse gets too short in the neck, and the shoulder no longer can move forward freely. The horse becomes afraid of the hand, and does not step into the contact. After a while, he must be ridden with strong legs, spurs and whip. Even then the horse is afraid to go forward because he has lost confidence in his natural tendency to go forward. The horse cannot reach under with the hind leg to support the back and strengthen his back muscles. Even the slightest weight of the rider gives the horse pain. The *Schwung,* which must be developed through the hind leg, cannot be sent freely over the back (the bridge between the back and front). The *Schwung*, which is so necessary for all gaits, figures, transitions, lateral work, pirouettes, passage, etc., to make them look powerful and effortless, disappears. The rider then tries to recover it through very strong hand aids, spurs and whip. The gaits deteriorate and become mechanical. The horse is not a partner but a slave and loses all his brilliance and charisma. This type of riding will work—at least temporarily—for a few horses and riders, but never for most of the horses and riders. This would be poison for them.

Some of the top riders and judges will object to this description, but someone must have the courage to speak up for the needs of horses and horsemanship. The best riders will understand and will thank those who uphold these standards, because they surely would like to be rewarded for having horses that go very willingly and will respond to very discreet aids.

For the so-called show trained horses, one can only feel sorry, for they have never felt complete partnership with their riders. Regardless of how successful they become in the show ring, I would not want to ride their horses, because they will be so difficult and mechanical. It is really not a nice feeling. When a rider tries to buy a horse like this and is told that he must be tougher with the horse to force him to execute certain figures, only makes me want to cry. This is also the reason why so many good horses are lost after a short time. Why are so many top horses taken out of top shows like World Championships or Olympics because of illnesses like colic, ulcers, nervous misbehavior or lameness? This happens when the rider increasingly exceeds the horse's limit, the closer the competition comes, instead of carefully building up the horse so that he does not get sour and sore, mentally or physically.

In classical dressage one should never abandon the commitment to train every day exactly according to the training scale. When practiced with the necessary endless patience the horse learns to react to the softest, almost invisible aids. The *Schwung* goes to the front and all exercises and gaits look powerful and brilliant. Horse and rider are partners in a harmony that is built up on the basis of mutual respect and trust, without the need for unnecessary force. The door to the front is open for him through a soft forward giving hand. Basic exercises are built up slowly but steadily toward the more difficult exercises. Everything flows harmoniously and powerfully. Even up to the Grand Prix, the relaxation is never lost. This correct, classical, patient daily training at home will produce a horse that is ready to go to a show any day, and perform with relaxation and confidence.

8.2 What is the point of competing?

It is important to remember that competing in a show means nothing more than showing the work that we are doing at home with the horse, in front of the judges. The judges' scores indicate to the rider whether his work is on the right track or not. We must always remember, however, that choosing to compete is our decision, not the horse's. So we must do everything in our power to reduce the extra stress that competing will inevitable impose on the horse, and to make the experience as pleasant and as safe as we can for him.

8.3 Getting the most out of it

Once you have decided to enter shows, you will get the most out of the experience with some careful planning, preparation, and effort. It should be enjoyable and rewarding. Unless you are showing for a client who pays you to present his horse, there is really no other reason than the enjoyment of it that leads you to the show grounds. It is worth the time to make things go well.

Planning the campaign

Months before the show season starts, the rider should sit together with the "show committee:" the owner, the instructor, and the trainer, if any. They have to decide which competitions the rider and his horse should enter and at what level they can do best. The horse should always be entered at one level below the one at which he can do very well at home. Thus, the show performance will not take an exceptional effort for the rider and the horse. The rider should understand that at the show he has to expect about 20% less than his usual riding performance, due to the negative influence of the show atmosphere.

Other considerations include whether the rider needs a reader, or whether the test can be ridden from memory (the latter is always the best solution, as it is easier to concentrate on the test without having to listen to the reader), and how the horse will be shipped to the show, and when.

Preparing the horse

The first show. The horse must be well prepared for his first time showing. In addition to the slow and patient daily work to build up the horse's training and condition, this includes exposure to new and different places. It is very hard for our horses to get used to new surroundings because of all the unknown things like flowers, letters, judges stands and much more, but especially the rider's nervousness, which the horse senses immediately. All these could spell danger for the horse, whom nature has conditioned to be fearful of the unfamiliar. Millions of years of evolution have programmed the horse to expect that changes in his surroundings could signal the presence of a predator. These instincts cannot be extinguished overnight. That is why it is necessary, especially for young horses, to consider the first shows as a training experience. Never try to force the horse to success. He should look forward to the next show and we have to let him grow into the show atmosphere, if we want to have a good show horse in the future.

As a general rule, as the show approaches the rider should not change his daily work, he continues the same work consistently, including lots of different patterns. He should not make himself and his horse upset; both should stay calm. If they have worked seriously during the whole year, there is no reason to panic! Although the test should be ridden through from start to finish a few times to get a sense of the rhythm and flow, a dressage test should not be practiced over and over, so that the horse ends up knowing the test better than the rider and does not wait for his aids. The rider should practice only parts of the test in order to determine the existing weaknesses and how they can possibly be "covered over" in the test. At home he should work on the root of the weakness and try to improve, so he can better show the horse's strong side in the next test.

In short, the best way to prepare for a show is to have a daily training program that produces a horse that is relaxed and has complete trust in his rider every single day of the year. Each day, the horse should be ridden to the limit but not over it. Such a horse will be ready to give his best performance every day, whether at home or on the show grounds. Thus, every show actually begins many months earlier, at home. Serious and focused work is necessary to bring the best out in both horse and rider.

The same standard should be applied to both the horse's and the rider's grooming and equipment. The horse's mane and tail, the tack, and the rider's show clothes and boots should always be so well maintained that we could go to a show at any time. Then all that needs to be done is to braid the mane. Actually, manes should be braided occasionally, even without going to a show. The horse will get used to it and the mane will fall better.

Show day

Loading. Loading should be practiced days and weeks before a horse show. This should be done by only a very experienced horseman. It is a very good help to have an easy loader that can be led on the trailer first, so the shying horse can follow. Horses that are difficult to load usually had bad experiences before, and a single bad experience will not soon be forgotten. The best way to produce an easy loader is to make sure that every loading experience, right from the start, is a good one. The first loading practice should take place at a time and in a place where everything is calm and unpressured. The challenge is to overcome the horse's understandable disinclination to place himself in that small and frequently dark space. Some horses, especially if they have already learned complete trust in their handler, will walk right on. If he is balky, the horse should be calmly and consistently given to understand that getting on the trailer is the only option for where he is going to go next. This may mean allowing him to stand for a time at the entrance to the trailer, with occasional urging to walk in. He should not be allowed to walk too far away from that spot, but under no circumstances should force be used to get the horse on the trailer.

Above: *A well-appointed trail-er.* Left: *The trailer hook-up must always be in good order and should be checked regular-ly. Photos by Jane Seigler.*

On the day of the show, preparations should begin early, especially if the horse is a difficult loader, as most people are in a hurry on show days and get nervous when the horse does not go into the trailer. The horse himself will get very tense and fright-ened. This is something we really do not need, because the horse should be at his best on the show day.

Of course, it goes without saying that our responsibility to the horse includes scrupulous attention to minimizing the risks of trailering. The interior of the trailer and the hitch should be well maintained and carefully inspected frequently.

Hay nets should not be hung too low, and must be checked regularly, because they will drop too low when empty, and the horse can get caught in it with his foot. The horse should never be trailered with saddle and bridle. It is not horseman-like, and it is dangerous for the equipment and for the horse. The heavier horse should always be loaded on the left side of the trailer. This should be also the case when trai-lering only one horse. Most roads in North America have a slight incline to the right.

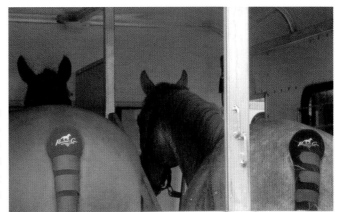

When loading only one horse, it should be standing on the left. When two horses are loaded, the heavier one should be on the left. Photo by Jane Seigler.

This means that centrifugal force might cause the horse or the trailer to become unbalanced while cornering, if too much weight is on the right side.

Make sure to arrive on the show ground early, and not at the last minute, which will make everybody including the horse nervous. The show stall should always be checked thoroughly for any dangerous condition. If the horse will be staying overnight on the show grounds, one person should be assigned the night watch. This person should always think of the horse first and should take very good care of it, ensuring a quiet, safe night with ample hay and water. If we expect an optimal performance of our horse, we must do our utmost to make him feel good.

If possible, a helper should go to the show office and organize everything, so the rider can concentrate exclusively on his horse and prepare for the competition and the warm-up. Nervous or inexperienced horses should be led around the show ground. The rider then becomes the "lead animal" for the horse, and the horse is quieter.

Everything on show day should be as familiar and as similar to everyday at home as it is possible to make it. Never use a new saddle or new bridles for the show. Also, never re-shoe the horse the day of or the day before the show. This would be like going to a dance competition with new shoes!

The warm-up

This is where the show is won or lost.

Getting the horse properly prepared and safely transported to the show grounds requires the team effort of the owner, instructor, trainer/rider and groom. At this point, the major responsibility falls on the rider.

Horse and rider should have ample time to prepare. This means being in the warm-up ring early enough. Enough time should be allotted to really focus on the warm-up. Only when the horse goes over the back, with a relaxed and active hind leg, will he be responsive to the aids, with all three gaits in the right rhythm and tempo, in harmony, exhibiting pride and brilliance in the test. This takes time and patience.

With actively engaged and slightly lower hind legs, the horse will automatically achieve a better elevation of the forehand." Rider: Eddo Hoekstra, in a perfect seat, his horse clearly in front of him. Photo by Roel Hoekstra.

Through slow warm-up exercises like posting trot, leg-yielding, lateral work, and lots of transitions, the horse becomes relaxed, active and in balance. Through this suppleness and activity of the hind legs, the horse will almost automatically come onto the aids and into a correct frame. This is called the "relative elevation," where the shoulders elevate, the neck arches and the poll is the highest point—all originating in an engaged and lowered hindquarter and a relaxed and swinging back.

Many riders forget that it is impossible to learn on the show grounds what has not been solidly and consistently achieved at home. This is another reason why we should enter the show at the level below what we are training at home. In the new surroundings, we have no chance of succeeding at something that we usually have trouble with at home.

I am reminded of the Olympic Games in Los Angeles in 1984. I had an excellent seat where I could see the main ring as well as the three warm-up rings that were set up on the race track. Thus, I had an excellent view of the warm-ups as well the tests. It was extremely hot, with temperatures of almost 100 degrees, and riders and horses both suffered. Consequently, riders were given lots of time to prepare their horses. Just before the show ring was the final warm-up arena, where the rider on deck could make final preparations, shine the boots, put on the tailcoat, etc. Before this one, there were three more warm-up rings, in which only one rider was allowed at any time. This means that riders had three warm-up rings before entering the main ring. For me, it was more interesting to watch the riders' warm-up than to observe the actual tests. I got the impression that many riders were trying to quickly teach their horses something that they would have to show in the show ring. In every successive ring, things got more and more intense, until they actually entered the main arena. All brilliance was drained from the horse, and we saw only a picture of tension and fatigue. The tired horse could only get through the test with very strong aids.

Of course one could also see excellent warm-ups—for example, from Dr. Reiner Klimke (who passed away much too soon). He began his work in the first warm-up ring with walking and trotting on a long-rein. In the next ring, he still rode relaxed movements, trot and canter, as well leg-yielding. In the third warm-up ring he worked on transitions in walk, trot and canter, followed by some more collected work like piaffe, passage, flying changes and pirouettes, but always with periods of rest, then complete halt. Then he would practice pieces of the test. Finally, in the last warm- up ring, he reviewed the whole test one last time in his mind, put on his coat, and rode into the stadium. There, Ahlerich went once more around the whole ring without showing excitement. The almost perfect test was the reward of an excellent, quiet and concentrated warm-up. I wish everyone could have seen this excellent warm-up. This was for me one of the nicest sights of my life that I will always carry around in my heart. I am very thankful to God for giving me the opportunity to see this.

Horses and riders must try very hard not to be influenced by the unfamiliar atmosphere on the show ground. This can manifest itself as nervousness of the rider and horse. Even if the horse was prepared very well at home, and the rider experienced, they may be a little more "backed off" at the show. This is just as true when the show is held at home, even more so. Suddenly the horse sees flowers, flags and many spectators that were not there yesterday; everything is strange for him and makes him frightened. Even though we do not have to travel and the horse can stay in his own stall, we do not have a big advantage. It is important that the rider stays calm and tries not to get infected by the hectic pace.

The horse should be warmed-up in exactly the same manner and routine as at home. Many times one sees riders prepare their horses completely differently on the show grounds from what they would normally do at home. The rider gets nervous and impatient when his horse does not perform immediately the things he can usually do at home. One should never forget that the horse also feels that something special is going on. We have to remember how sensitive the horses are to our own emotions. This underscores the importance of having a regular work program that is scrupulously followed at home. By following this same plan on the show grounds, the horse takes comfort from this bit of something familiar in the strange place and is more relaxed.

When too many horses are in the warm-up ring, the rider should try to go to some other quiet spot where the horse can be worked quietly. He should not let himself be influenced by riders who put their horses on the bit right away. Those horses are never truly on the aids.

When a rider gets on the horse and immediately puts him on the bit, the horse cannot step confidently into the hand of the rider, but instead comes behind the bit and escapes the aids. We know that one of two things will result: the warm-up will go badly, and the test will be a disaster, or what we observe in the test are mechanical movements, not true, gymnastically correct ones. Even though all the movements may be shown, the supple and elastic brilliance that should be shown in the test is missing.

Many times one sees riders who, almost immediately after mounting, try to go right away into the most collected, difficult movements. This leads to fights with the horse, which will lead to tense gaits and a stressed horse. First of all this is not a very nice sight, and gives spectators a bad impression of this rider. One has to ask how he rides his horses at home where nobody can see him, when he rides in this rough and impatient way at the show, where many people can see him. No rider should take this type of riding as an example. No matter how the horse presents himself in the test, no one can have a nice feeling for the horse, after witnessing this kind of riding during the warm-up. It makes one wonder why these riders are riding in the first place, when it looks like they hate their horses.

We all like to see nice rides, just as we like to have nice rides. We should always be fair to our horse, be it at home, during the warm-up, or in the dressage ring. This fairness starts with the quality of our seat. Unfortunately, in the warm-up rings and in the test one sees many very imperfect seats: riders with high knees and heels, and constant kicking with legs and spurs. The Schwung gets interrupted with very hard hands. All aids are exaggerated. The horse's balance is disturbed by a constantly moving and bouncing torso. The horses' backs are very tight. One hardly sees riders with a good seat anymore, and that's why all the movements are stiff, why horses are behind the bit and will only go forward with strong spur aids, their true beauty and pride suppressed. The aids should be discreet, so that you can hardly see them. But one very rarely sees horses being ridden with very soft aids.

Sometimes, it is sad to say, the discomfort we inflict on our horses rises to the level of intentional or reckless cruelty. The pressures of competition can make some riders forget their humanity, and vent their tension and anxiety on their poor horses, who already feel and are no doubt being affected by the riders' emotion. Nobody should ever have to go to the steward and complain about a rider being very rude and rough with the horse. Sometimes stewards will not do anything because this rough rider is a very successful one, and the steward doesn't want to get involved with him. Such a rough rider—it doesn't make any difference who it is - should not be on a show ground. A rider who is cruel to his horse e.g., because he spurs the horse so hard in the test that the horse has blood stains on both sides, should be disqualified in the warm-up ring or after the test. It is regrettable that sometimes nobody stops this rough (torturing) riding, neither a steward, nor a judge, nor somebody from the FN or the FEI. They should be banned from riding in future shows. This kind of rough riding has given dressage riding a very bad reputation with riders, spectators, and riders from other disciplines, who all condemn this as cruelty to animals.

If our old Masters could see this, they would turn in their graves. They would have never allowed us to do anything like this, because the well-being of the horses was always the main priority. Dressage riding should be a partnership based on mutual respect for many years. Riders who think otherwise give a bad example of our beautiful sport for spectators and upcoming generations.

Many will crucify me because I have written this, but someone has to have the courage to say what a shame it is to see what is being done in the daily work and at the shows with our poor horses. Thank God that so far there are only few for whom the only way to success is through rough riding and punishment. I know also that those

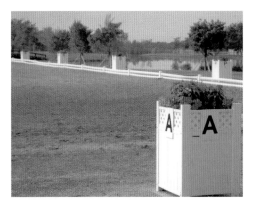

If the horse is more comfortable on the left track, one should enter the arena from the left. The letter A should be left on the rider's right side. If the horse is better on the right track, it is better to enter from the right, this time leaving the letter A on the left. In both cases the rider can easily find the center line, without having to wiggle himself toward it.

very few riders sometimes recognize that they are on the wrong path and try to go back to the classical, gymnasticizing way of training. However, staying on this correct path can be very hard for them, and they often fall back into the old mistake of taking short cuts. One sees more and more of this way of riding, which leads to rapid yet mechanical successes.

Both during the warm-up and in the dressage ring, riders should present harmonious pictures that are a pleasure to watch. This we owe to our partners, the horses, who give us their all.

Now we come to the test. The rider should go on both reins around the whole ring so the horse has the possibility to see the new surroundings, with some transitions and complete halts. The halts should be made as they will be required in the test—i.e., out of walk, trot or canter. The horse should be allowed to stand long and quietly in the halt. When the rider takes his reins in the left hand to salute and the horse immediately moves off, this is a sign that the rider either did not take enough care in the training to let the horse stand long enough after the halt, or (and this is most often the reason) the horse is frightened because of too much force and framing. At this time, never show any movements that are not required in the test or that your horse does not do well. The judge will immediately see this. We do not want him to conclude that we are showing a "ringer," and we certainly do not want to show him ahead of time what trouble we might have during the test. It is very important to ride the test in a way that will showcase the strengths of the horse, and that will de-emphasize his weakness.

The test should be ridden very harmoniously, as if horse and rider were floating from point to point. Every figure should be ridden exactly at the required spot and be correctly executed. This again shows the great importance of a correct seat to enable the rider to give correct and almost invisible aids at precisely the right moment.

Until the rider has left the ring, he must fully concentrate, especially on the first and the last halt. These are the first and last impressions that the judges remember. Between the first and last halt, he must ride every step of the test as preparation for the each of the movements. This is what produces tests that are seamless and flowing. When the rider freezes or "goes to sleep" between the movements, and the movements come as interruptions in that sleep walk, the horse is surprised by the movements and the test appears sporadic and jerky. Only with such a concentrated performance, with ample impulsion, can the rider expect a good score.

Many riders slap their horses aggressively after the final halt. Although the intent is to praise the horse, it appears almost like a spanking. Also, some riders are so impressed with themselves that one sees them jumping around like clowns. Can't we show our happiness without these excessive displays that our horses cannot appreciate and may even be frightened by? When a soccer player shoots a goal and gets all excited and rips off his shirt, he gets a yellow card. Two yellow cards lead to elimination for the player. Shouldn't we have the same—or better—ethics when displaying happiness with our rides?

After the ride, the rider should dismount immediately and lead his horse to cool him off. He should lead the horse back to the stable where good, clean bedding allows the horse to feel secure and comfortable, even in unfamiliar surroundings.

8.4 A word about freestyles

Freestyles in dressage are enjoying a huge increase in interest and popularity. This is good, as it will help to bring more interest to the sport. Freestyles give the rider much more freedom to express his horse's particular talents and style. With this freedom, however, comes responsibility.

A pair of very nice final halt/salutes by riders Theresa Doherty and Eddo Hoekstra.

The principle of the staircase of the training must always have priority over the artistic aspect. Rhythm, relaxation, Schwung, as well as harmony between rider and horse must be the top priority. As beautiful as a freestyle performance is for the judges and the audience, it must not resemble a circus performance. For instance, piaffe pirouettes and half pass in the passage can only look good when the horse executes a very natural, relaxed, and not forced piaffe and passage. All those exercises require utmost strength, flexibility, Schwung and suppleness. In spite of the difficulty, the relaxation of the horse must be visible. If this is not the case and the horse does not have either a good piaffe or passage, these exercises will only make the horse more frightened and tense. The piaffe and passage will get worse, not better. They will evolve into a bad performance with extremely strong aids, which does not help the image of dressage riding. Something else is beginning to "creep in."

It makes me very happy that the rider is no longer allowed to perform triple pirouettes in the freestyle (which are very hard on the horse's hocks, joints and tendons). I am also glad that the rules now encourage the horse to be ridden at least one straight stride between the pirouette from the half pass, to confirm the straightness necessary for true collection before the pirouette and the balance after it, rather than allowing the horse to be thrown, out of balance, from one to the other.

8.5 *Pressures on the professional*

It is not easy for an instructor to also compete in a show, especially if he is working for a stable from which many horses and riders are competing. If the instructor also competes, he will not be able to give his students his full attention. Something will suffer. If he really wants to take good care of his riders, he will not be able to concentrate on his own riding. This was the reason why I stopped showing, so that I could give my full attention to the lessons and the riders at shows. After all, they are the ones who pay us. Too many of our colleagues try to do both, compete and take care of their students at shows. It is much better to pick different shows for students and for your own showing.

It is a different thing when you work for a private owner. Then you only need to concentrate on the owner and his horses. Often the owner does not even ride himself, but the rider still is under a lot of pressure, as you are expected to produce success, which is very important for the owner who may have very good and expensive horses for his hobby. It is expected that ribbons and prize money will be won. (Incidentally, etiquette dictates that ribbons and prize money go to the owner, whereas the rider gets the trophy.) Thus, even when you do not have too many riders to take care of, the pressure to be successful is always there.

9

the judge

9.1 The judge's important role

"Judges are the Guardians of the Art of Riding"[6]

Christoph Hess

Judges complete our Circle. They are very, very important and have great influence on the sport and the horses. As with the breeders and trainers, we would have no sport without the efforts and dedication of our judges. The most amazing thing about judges is that they even do it! It is hard to imagine a more difficult way to make very little money—sitting from morning to night in a small booth or a smelly trailer, (seldom in a nice judging gazebo), watching endless repetitions of usually mediocre performances, freezing in the cold or baking in the sun with only short and infrequent breaks. Ultimately, they do this for the love of the sport. It is, of course, a position where one gets a lot of prestige and favorable attention, but the attention can also be unfavorable if the judging does not work out well.

9.2 What judges can do

Judges have the responsibility to tell riders whether they are on the correct or incorrect path in training their horses. Like an instructor, the judge's main function is to give advice, but unlike the instructor, he can only score and judge what he sees during a particular test. Advice is limited to the few comments written at the bottom of the score sheet, and through the scores for the movements. While the judge has the additional duty of placing the horses in order for the awarding of ribbons, the major

---

[6] See Appendix E for an interview with Christoph Hess

impact that he has on the sport is through the signals and messages that he communicates to the rider through the marks and written comments at the end of the score sheet.

When scoring a test, the judge is compelled to score the individual performance presented to him at that moment. The scoring cannot reflect an outstanding ride last week. Although it can and should acknowledge improvement through increasing scores over time, the best scores cannot be given to work that remains flawed.

The judge can and must advise the rider of all mistakes that result from incorrect training. However, because it is not the duty of the judge to tell the rider how to train his horse, these should be framed as general suggestions about how the rider has diverged from the right path and how to return to the right path.

Ideally, every judge should give the same marks and similar comments. With consistent judging, the rider can understand when the ride was better, because it is reflected in the scores. However, opinions can slightly diverge on how one could help the rider and his horse correct the mistakes. Therefore specific prescriptions should be avoided because rider and horse may get confused when different judges recommend different solutions.

9.3 *What judges can't do*

It is important for a judge to identify and describe mistakes and problems in the horse's training, but he cannot or may not always be able to tell the rider how he should train his horse. The judge, regardless of how good he is, sees mistakes but he cannot feel them and, in fact, may not have trained many horses to the level he is judging.

I often think of the late *Landstallmeister* Dr. Gustav Rau, who was one of our best judges. Even though he only rode in hunts, he had a great eye for recognizing every little mistake. Nevertheless, he would always say: "seeing and recognizing is not like training and teaching," which requires many years of experience to be able to recognize the constantly changing situation and feeling, and to adjust the aids to each situation.

A nice judging gazebo with an unobstructed view of the center line and all the rest, thanks to the side windows. This is Cheval Farm, in Wadsworth, Ohio, owned by Richard and Brenda Aughenbaugh

9.4 Rewarding fundamentally flawed performances

The judge should never overlook mistakes that reveal that the horse has been "mistrained." This is especially true when any or all three gaits are insufficient or when no walk is shown at all. It is fundamentally wrong when a rider enters the arena with a horse that is soaked in sweat. The horse should be warmed-up in a manner that allows him to remain relaxed and willing to stand still during the salute, and not what we saw so many times during the Olympics in Athens. This is a sign that the horse lacks fundamental relaxation (the first element of the Training Scale) or that not enough attention was paid to the halt in the training.

General Horst Niemack and Dr. Gustaf Rau (the mentor and initiator of riding after World War II) were two of the best judges in Germany in my time. Both always stated that judges should not look for mistakes alone, but must judge on the basis of a horse's general impression.

They preferred by far to see the rider's appropriate and skilful correction after the horse made a mistake, while maintaining a lot of *Schwung* and power in the three gaits and all exercises. The degree of relaxation indicated whether the horse showed the fundamental characteristics of a dressage horse. They would consistently place such a horse in front of others who lacked the correct rhythm and *Schwung* and had a tight back and were not at all relaxed. Even though those horses performed all the movements, they did everything mechanically.

When a tense or mechanically moving horse gets placed in front, or among the best, or even receives high marks from a judge, there is something wrong. This is not a good influence on dressage riding. Those marks and placings should be reserved for those riders who can show three clear and correct gaits, good transitions, relaxation, and correct and effective seat and the aids. A mechanical type of riding will never lead to perfection and should never become an example for our young riders. When those riders and horses have to win, because (for example) they are the only ones to show all the movements and exercises, they should be ranked on top, but never with high marks. Riders who come home from shows with high scores will naturally believe that they are close to the right track. The big wake-up call comes when they arrive at international shows or the Olympics. This means that it is up to our judges to lead our riders back on to the correct methods of training. I know that a judge must be brave to give low marks, but we have to show even the top riders what the right way is. I am sure our top riders will be not be happy with this judge in the beginning, and will say that this judge has no idea. However, I also know that the judge's role is to help these riders recognize that they are on the wrong track. Honest, ethical judging will help lead these riders back to the correct training methods, based on the well-being of the horse.

9.5 What judges should cultivate by rewarding

For a detailed description of what the properly moving horse should look like, see Appendix F, by Col. Hans von Heydebreck.

The most important quality of the horse is three correct gaits. The walk is the hardest movement to ride correctly. It should be free and lively, without rushing. It should be long and quiet and have a correct four-beat pattern. Jogging, excessively marching, ambling and the Spanish walk are mistakes caused by the horse hollowing his back and thus not stepping correctly into the hand of the rider. These mistakes are initiated with the young horse and are very hard to correct. Whoever started the young horse, did not give it enough confidence to step clearly forward in the walk. Often these horses were forced into a frame much too early. Their shoulders are thereby blocked, the front leg cannot reach forward but has to go unnaturally up and down, and the hind leg is not able to step under his body to support the back. The horse has to hollow his back, and the lightest rider's weight is already too heavy for the horse, making him tight and giving him pain. The quality of the walk also gets lost through hands that are too strong and work backwards. This is the reason why we do not see more correct walks in the higher levels. The rider then loses points in the test because one of the three gaits is not correct. Many a big competition is lost because of a bad walk and this is how it should be.

The trot should be a clear two-beat rhythm. It should have *Schwung*, and be free in the shoulder. The horse should go clearly over the back. The horse's nose should always be in front of the vertical and the poll should always be the highest point. In the working trot, the frame should be a little longer. In the medium and extended trot the frame of the neck should get even longer (not shorter), in order to free the shoulder. This allows the front leg to swing out. The nose shows where the front leg should land.

Driving of the hind legs develops power and collection, and the created impulsion can be sent as *Schwung* over the back to the front. This is how we can recognize a good back-mover. The rider will appear to have his horse in front of him and that he is riding up-hill. The medium and extended gaits can be only as good as the collection was successful. A horse will be a leg-mover when he gets too short in the neck (i.e., gets "absolute" elevation, or "absolute" framing, or is "put on the bit"). The front legs will be tight and will come unnaturally high, slapping hard back down to the ground. The hind legs struggle to keep the horse in balance, and can only take short steps that do not cover any ground. In the collected trot, the horse should clearly lower his hind leg. The hip, knee and hock develop more angle and thus create more elevation in the front.

This is "relative" elevation, not "absolute" elevation. The latter results more from a lifting of the neck with the hand than a lowering of the hind

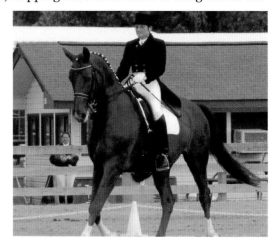

Jane Seigler on her horse Karakter in relative elevation.

legs. Absolute elevation gives the horse a hollow back, and the power and *Schwung* created by the hind legs cannot flow freely over the back, withers, neck, poll, and mouth into the hand of the rider. The front legs go up and down, but do not cover more ground. In the test, the horse takes a very long time to go across the diagonal because of the unnatural up and down of the front legs. This may look spectacular to the uneducated, but it does not have anything to do with the natural rhythm of a powerful trot.

In correct, relative, elevation the nose can come closer to the vertical the more collected the trot gets. The horse must remain very free and the poll must stay the highest point. Far too often we see a working trot at the higher levels, instead of a true collected trot, because when the rider asks for collection, the trot becomes passage-like. The horse escapes the aids and escapes the collection, which indicates that the hind legs are not swinging through, over the back. The horse should be able to show a clear difference between collected trot and passage. This can only happen when he is stepping confidently with the hind leg over the back into the rider's hand.

This is also the reason why one sees very few good piaffe-passage and passage-piaffe transitions. These problems started at the lower levels in the transitions from walk to trot and trot to walk, from lengthening back to working trot, and from medium and extended trot back to collected trot. In the transitions within and between gaits, if the rider was not soft with his hands and did not make the hind legs lively not slower, the *Schwung* and the rhythm will get lost. Typically, these transitions are ridden with too hard a hand and leg and spur aids that are too visible. For example, in the transitions to medium or extended gaits, the riders push the horses like they are shot out of a cannon, instead of just thinking of lengthening the frame while keeping the horse always on the aids. The horse gets pushed away from the aids, and is not enough under control. As a result, in the transition back to more collection, the half halts do not come through, but escapes in the second or third vertebra, the neck becomes shorter, and the nose ends up more behind the vertical, or is even pulled to the chest. These mistakes in the basics carry forward to the highest levels. It is the responsibility of the judge to mark the movement down—no matter how good the lengthening—if there is no correct downward transition back to working trot or collection.

The correct canter must have three clear beats. The rider should appear to ride "uphill," with a round and floating movement over the back. The hock must be elastic. The horse should show a powerful stride while the hoof beats remain soft and almost noiseless. Again, the highest point must be the poll, and the neck must rise out of the withers in front of the rider. The horse must be straight, absolutely soft in the hand, must step confidently to the hand and always must be well relaxed. When the horse is not straight, it cannot generate a correct foot sequence. The horse can only be straight when he is very supple, forward, and responds easily to all aids. When the horse is straight, it will be easy to ride corners and circles, and to develop and execute voltes, pirouettes, counter-canter, half-pass, even in zig-zag, flying changes, etc. The horse should show powerful extended gaits, with the neck visibly stretched, and then come back easily to the collection anywhere the rider might ask, in a powerful, precise and smooth manner, without any resistance. In the collection, the horse should elevate his neck and head through lowering of the hind legs and look proud, while always being ready to respond instantly to the aids for a medium or extended canter.

Good marks should never be given when the horse opens his mouth, sometimes even in spite of an excessively tight noseband. (This should, in fact, be penalized by the stewards in the warm-up ring because this is unfair and gives the horse lots of pain and interferes with his breathing.) The same is true when the horse goes behind the vertical, or pushes the tongue out of his mouth and over the bit, because of excessively hard hands. This problem is often created by riding young horses too much in collected canter, resulting in stiff hocks and tight backs. Young horses need good forward riding to improve the canter and develop *Schwung*, (without, of course, going over the limit of the horse). *Schwung* is an important component of any collected canter. It is possible to ride with *Schwung* without collection, but never to ride collection without *Schwung*.

High marks should never be given when the horse's neck is over-shortened. These horses can be seen in the warm-up ring, with their riders forcing them to give in through a hard hand pulling to the left and to the right. When the neck is too short and the horse goes behind the bit it is impossible to show nice, correct and relaxed movements. A horse that is ridden this way can never go over the back. His blocked shoulder stops every forward movement. The door in the front is shut, and the hind legs have to go either high or wide, because the movement over the back to the front is so impossible. Most such horses have a four-beat canter with very short strides, where the *Schwung* is lost. The hind legs push, but they don't carry, because they have too much trouble keeping the balance. The horse's hocks and back are tight and stiff, and the gait is not "springy." The horse has to put his legs down immediately and cannot jump under. How can one ever show such a horse in medium or extended trot or canter? How can such a horse execute a floating pirouette or correct flying changes, when it is in a four-beat canter, and constantly disturbed by the rider's hand?[7]

Throughout the performance, it all comes down to how important it is to have good *Schwung* and relaxation. In my time we had an all day competition in which we had to take a small jump after the test in the morning, in both directions, so the judge could see if the horse was tense or relaxed.[8]

---

[7] See my book **Dressage in Harmony**, page 245 (Conclusion), for a description of a horse unable to perform one tempo changes.

[8] In the afternoon we had the main test. All horses had to go together in single file, under the command of the judge, to determine how the horse behaved in a group. At the end, all riders could show their horse's strength individually, but only figures that were part of the relevant test were allowed. The morning and afternoon tests were judged together. If the horse had the best score in the morning but behaved poorly in the afternoon, it could not win this competition.

After three refusals the rider and the horse were disqualified, no matter how good the test was. How the horse jumped over the fence determined either good or bad notes. This made it impossible for us to drill the horse exclusively for the test, as we also had to train it over jumps. This was a way to determine whether the horse had been trained purely mechanically. It would show if the horse was ridden correctly over his back or if it showed too much tension. I would just love to see the horses today who are trained with "Rollkur" go over a jump after their test. I am convinced that a net would have to be put up about one hundred yards behind the jump in order to catch horse and rider!

It is too bad that they scratched the jump from the test. The practice was dropped because of complaints by those riders who rode only dressage and nothing else. The horses became mechanical. The same happens today. Some riders would like to see elimination of the walk in the Grand Prix test. Isn't the walk one of the three gaits; and isn't a clear and correct gait important for a dressage horse? Again, this comes from riders whose horses are so frightened and tense and that they do not walk. Why don't we scratch the halt and salute from the tests, because so many top riders have such a big problems with the halt? Why not let the riders show only what they do best?

Where will this type of riding lead us? For sure, not to a dressage that is built up on equal respect and trust, where the horse reacts to the softest and almost invisible aids, whether they are forwards, sideways or backwards. Instead, everything will be tight and stiff, and the feeling of the horse will be lost.

This is also the reason why so many riders do not have a correct seat. Poor training has produced many horses that are leg-movers and not back-movers. When a horse is a leg mover, it does not have a swinging back. Riders who sit on leg movers work a lot with their hands to try to achieve softness. Their legs are constantly in motion, trying to bring the hind legs more under. Their knees and heels are too high. In the flying changes and in the pirouettes they move their legs almost into the soft spot in the flank. The outside leg is much too far back, thus the horse is overbent, gets behind the vertical and the whole movement gets "sticky." In the piaffe and passage the legs are not on the girth where they can drive forwards, but rather where the supporting and sideways driving spots are. The riders use the spurs as a substitute for their legs and leave spur marks. A horse that is ridden in this manner, even if it can do the movements, is like a dressage machine. This has nothing to do with classical dressage.

I have refrained from listing all the mistakes that make it impossible for the horse to move correctly. The judges know them anyway, but they have become used to this type of riding, because to a large degree, they only see these types of horses. The FEI rules are very clear about how a correct horse should move and look. Unfortunately, we have completely drifted away from these standards. Only when the judges stick to the rules can we find the way back to a correct riding that is also human and humane.

Once a mistake has been created, it is very hard to correct but, more importantly, it opens up the way for more mistakes to creep in. If judges overlook the problems through the levels and still give high marks, they are not doing the riders, horses and the whole sport of dressage a favor, for they will often perpetuate well beyond the original problem. More and more mistakes will be made and the result will be completely different from what we expect from classical dressage training. We want to see clear, powerful and harmonious gaits, good transitions, relaxation, as well as a correct seat and aids on the part of the rider. Anything less will never lead to perfection and should never be an example for our young riders.

9.6 Reacting to being judged—sportsmanship

While it is best if all scoring is consistent, we do not live in a perfect world, and riders, owners and instructors must be aware that variations in scoring will always occur. If judged by two or more judges for the same test, it is likely that the scores will differ, because the judges will see movements from different angles—the half-pass viewed from the front will look considerably different when viewed from the side, and so on. Also, judges may place different importance on some qualities. Finally, judges are under a certain amount of subtle pressure to keep scores relatively high, and individuals respond to this pressure in different ways. The ride that was greatly improved from one week to the next may score the same because the first judge was lenient, while the second stood by his principles.

It is very common for the rider (and his instructor) to dismiss poor marks because of some perceived bias on the part of the judge. (He likes only warmbloods, etc.). This is even said at the Olympics, with dressage being no more immune to sour grapes than ice skating or gymnastics. But the rider should look at every mark, take all of them seriously, and consider how they can help improve his training in the future. If the rider does not appreciate this, it is his fault, he will continue as before and cannot be helped.

Every rider should first be critical with himself, and recognize that the judge may well be right. Even if the judge were biased against your horse, any low mark for a poorly shaped circle, a late transition, resistance against very strong aids, etc., is a clear and simple statement about clear mistakes. They need to be fixed—not by force or by riding the same figure over and over again, hoping that it will improve—but with lots of patient work and understanding. One has to find the root of the mistake and not just treat the symptoms. You cannot fix a tooth by putting on a crown if the root is infected.

If a rider feels strongly that a particular judge is biased or otherwise difficult, then he has the easy recourse of staying home. There are many shows, and judges are booked months and months in advance, so it is not difficult to avoid them. While we would like to think that the ethics of sportsmanship would prevent this type of behavior, it is still far superior to going to a show and complaining constantly. My old master always told us if you go to a horse show to demonstrate what you have done at home, you have to respect the judgment of the judge. If not, you better stay home. It is a difficult job, and if riders are always protesting, judges will soon ask "why in the world do I put up with this?"

In addition, dressage show management is largely done through the tireless efforts of dressage associations and is often a volunteer effort. Most recognized shows will gladly take your comments on judging, footing, secretary, food, and so on, through the mail, but show management has far too much to do on the day of a show to deal with petty complaints of riders who scored less well than they feel entitled to.

Owners or sponsors should never do anything to create a conflict of interest for the judge. Even though the rules prohibit the most overt forms of "bribery" or impropriety, the judge should not be put in the difficult position of having to offend the owner by refusing small gifts or favors. The best plan is to show good performances if you want the judge to give good scores and placing.

9.7 Credibility and the appearance of propriety

First and foremost, the judge must be well educated and well prepared. He must know the tests exactly, and should have experience riding and training horses through the level that he is judging. He must know what the objective of the test is, why the movements that are shown at this level are called for, and must make remarks appropriate for the level of training expected. For any low mark, the judge has to be explicit as to why it was given. He should under no circumstances make bad remarks about the rider to the scribe.

The judge needs to know the precise order of all the movements, and where the movements are divided for scoring. It is ultimately the judge's responsibility to ensure that the recorded marks and comments are correct and legible.

Beyond that, it goes without saying that the judge must be scrupulously impartial and fair. Unfortunately, one can see even at the Olympics that judges forgive a top rider a mistake more easily than other riders. Moreover, scoring should not go up and down because of the importance of the show or the rider. Fairness requires that scoring be consistent across all types of shows.

Our breeders provide us with excellent horses with three excellent gaits, beauty and charisma. It is up to the riders and trainers to maintain these characteristics, to get them under forceless control and to make it more beautiful. They must recognize what is wrong and right. What good is it for a rider to win many shows by having schooled and re-schooled his horses for a single test, as though he were engaged in training dogs? We should not see dressage machines, but rather riders who have fun and have a smile on their faces, and horses that have fun during their work, both exhibiting a harmonious unity and partnership through mutual trust and respect.

I have been asked many times why I have not become a judge. I would certainly not give high marks to horses who are trained mechanically (what I call "poodle dressage"), showing no charm and brilliance. If I were a judge, only the first three finishers would like me, while the others would say that I have no idea about what is correct. Pretty soon we will have no judges, and the riders will have to judge each other. You can easily imagine what would happen: they would kill each other.

We have to be very thankful there are people willing to be a judge.

10 conclusion

With this book I have tried to explain to everyone who is part of the Circle around our horses what responsibility they have toward our horses. The horse depends on us and we have the duty to make his unnatural life with us easier. The horse will reward our love and caring with loyalty and devotion.

Our **Breeders** supply us with very good horses. Without them, we would have no equestrian sports at all.

The **Owners** (Sponsors) give the **Riders**, **Trainers** and **Instructors** financial support to develop the horse to his best. It is, in turn, their duty and responsibility to make the horse brilliant and expressive of his own joy, by showing off his power and athleticism, as well as his ability to react willingly to even the most discreet and almost invisible aids.

The author with his wife Heide, his psychological and physical support in life.

The **_Groom_** takes on the task of making the horse feel safe and secure, and sees to his basic physical and emotional needs.

The **_Show Committee_** consists of owners, trainers, riders, instructors and grooms whose mission is to send horses and riders to shows, fit and able to do well and have a positive experience. The show committee should develop a culture of respect for the role of shows and the role of judges in providing guidance in the training. It must be a part of that culture that the judge's comments are taken in the spirit of helping with the training. And it goes without saying that all riders should be fair to and supportive of other riders, and should never make critical comments. We only need to remember that—no matter how good we are now—we've all been in bad places along the way!

Judges are the guardians of the art of riding. They show the rider and the trainer if they are on the right track or if something went wrong in the training. They must not shirk their responsibility to stop cruelty and abuse.

If this book has helped in any way to make life easier for horse and rider, it was worthwhile writing it.

history of the Trakehner breed

by Harry Zimmerman

The story of the Trakehner breed is an object lesson in the ravages of war and the incredible depth of devotion true horseman will show to their horses in the face of incredible horrors and hardship.

Before World War II, the Trakehner was the largest and most influential breed in Germany. The Trakehner is a warm-blooded horse whose roots go back to the twelfth century and the knights in shining armor. The knights who conquered the area that was later known as East Prussia brought with them their heavy war horses that had been bred to carry a man and full suit of armor into battle. Heavy mounts were in fashion. But in 1503 at the battle of Naples, Condottore Saguo de Cordova used more agile, light horses of Spanish origin and turned the battle to his advantage, and a new era began.

In 1732 King Frederick the Great chose the best horses from his royal breeding farm in order to establish a new stud farm at Trakehnen. The objective was a program of selective breeding of horses with endurance and a long, ground-covering gait. In the 1800's, a few top quality English Thoroughbred bloodlines were introduced with the goal of refining the Trakehner. The nerve and endurance of the Thoroughbred was desired, but care was taken to maintain the even temperament, substance and other qualities of the Trakehner. Further refinement and elegance in the breed came from the introduction of a few carefully selected Arabian stallions. The Trakehner was used as a military horse in time of war, and as a sport horse in time of peace.

Tempelhüter was undoubtedly the best known stallion of the Trakehner breed.

The breed was centered at stud farms in Trakehnen and East Prussia, in what is now Poland and Russia. Before the 20th century, horses born in the main breeding stud of Trakehnen were called Trakehners, with the brand of a half elk antler on the right hind leg. Foals born through private breeders outside of the main stud were called East Prussians (*Ostpreussen*), and were branded with double antlers on the left hind leg. At its largest, the main breeding farm had 18,000 mares. After 1787 they were organized in four herds of different colors: black, brown, chestnut and mixed. One of the best-known stallions was Tempelhueter, whose monument stood in front of the house of the Landstallmeister (the State Stud Director) in Trakehnen. In 1945 this monument was brought to Moscow and now stands in front of the horse museum there. A copy, made in 1974 through the efforts of Ostpreussen horse lovers, now stands in front of the horse museum in Verden/Aller in Germany.

Eventually, the breeding and riding of cavalry horses became the main industry in Prussia. Breeders in the area took their mares to the Government Stallion Station. (At this time, private breeders did not stand their own stallions.)

Before World War II the State Stud Director in East Prussia had the foresight to export breeding stock to western Germany. This probably saved the breed (which had grown to 25,000 horses) from extinction during the war. When the Soviets closed in on Trakehnen, the Prussians gathered their precious horses and fled towards safety in the west. The horror story, which followed, became known as the **Treck**. It was midwinter, the snow was deep and broodmares were heavy with foal. The Soviet troops were burning their homes and farms behind them and the Russian planes were machine gunning from the air. The Prussians could not stop when the mares foaled or horses went lame. The nightmare continued for two and one half months—a 1400 mile exodus of horses and humans. When they arrived at the shores of the frozen Baltic Sea and the only escape was across the treacherous expanse of ice, they forged ahead, at times galloping to stay ahead of ice breaking behind them. Thousands perished.

At last they limped into West Germany, fewer than 800 skeletons with open wounds from shrapnel and with burlap bags frozen to their feet. Even with a supply of oats, many died due to the lack of hay. Only the hardiest survived. The remnants of a once royal breed had undergone the greatest endurance test of all times. The parents of the author of this story left their homeland with eight Trakehner horses and three wagons. They arrived in West Germany with a broken down carriage and one lame gelding.

The post war years were spent rebuilding and re-establishing the Trakehner breed. Because every surviving Trakehner carried the brand of the double elk antler on the left hip, it made the task easier. Before long the Trakehner began to reappear as a winner at the Olympics and international competitions. The Trakehner's movement, coupled with its presence and temperament set it apart from other breeds.

thoughts, musings and words to live by

Where ability ends, brutality begins.

We are the ones who make the horses good or bad. When we are good, the horses are good, when we are bad, the horses are bad.

No partnership can be good when it is built on fear.

I know for sure that all our horses will go to Heaven, because of their kindness and forgiveness. I can not say this with certainty of all riders. Once there, our horses may well ride us, so we better be good.

Our horses are the most beautiful and finest creatures that God created, and He gave them to serve us. But we must not destroy their beauty and pride by making them into our slaves.

While we love our horses and do everything in our power for them, we can never be a replacement for what they would enjoy in the wild.

Our horses will do everything for us when we show them through the correct aids, given at the right moment, so that they can understand. They are our best teachers. It is not the horse's fault when he makes a mistake. We have to learn from the horse and his reaction to our aids. The horse's behavior and reactions are his language that we must learn in order to understand him fully.

Calm, forward and straight.

The horse feels your deepest feelings, both positive and negative. The horse will react accordingly.

Even the best trainer needs years of hard work, the help of an experienced teacher, and patience, until he is successful.

Every horse, like any human being, has weaknesses and strengths that must be taken into consideration.

If you would like to ride a good horse, you have to be good yourself.

Trust one can not force, one must work on it and earn it.

The trust between the rider and the horse should never be put at risk through impatient and rough reactions. Once the trust is lost, it may well be lost for good.

The horse will reward your love and caring with his endless loyalty and devotion.

One can not humanize the horse because horses will always be horses.

In the German language, the word rider means knight. Any rider, therefore, has the duty to be chivalrous to his horse and his fellow human beings.

One should only ride over fences that the horse can clear without getting hurt.

If you approach an obstacle with fear, your horse will refuse. Will power and trust are necessary for jumping, for dressage, and for all other forms of riding.

The horse must trust and respect you, but he should never fear you.

Dressage means bringing two different living creatures together in harmony, without any force. Two soul—one thought.

Giving and being soft is much harder than pulling.

We must always open the door in the front through soft and giving aids.

Soft but not loose, a loose rein can also be a harsh rein.

The less aids we can see, the better our horse will react to them.

Less but good is better than much and bad.

We have to go to the limit but never over.
More driving than receiving (1/2 lb. in the hand, 1 ½ lb. driving).

Every mistake was created long before it shows and has to be corrected at its root.

By picking up the reins we have to remind ourselves that we are now in contact with the most sensitive part of the horse—his mouth.

We have to show the horse what we would like to do, but we have to allow him to do it.
If you go to a horse show you have to trust the judge's score.

A horse will be always a horse but the rider not always a rider.

98% of all mistakes are made by the rider.

The horse does not make a mistake on purpose.

Before you punish your horse, you must ask yourself: do I need the punishment?

The best aids will not be successful if they are not given at the right moment.

In the eye of the horse one recognizes his soul.

We have to start with soft aids and make them stronger only when it is necessary.

You must turn your horse into your partner, not into your slave.

A partnership can only be built upon mutual respect and trust.

Dressage is a matter of trust.

First the rider has to control himself before he can control his horse.

First, there was the rider. Out of his experience the riding instructor evolved over time.

appendix c

ethics and morals for professional riders

by Guenther Festerling
translation by Lynne Sprinsky

Editors' note: This document generally is of universal import. However, certain references that are peculiar to the system for training and licensing professional riding teachers in the Federal Republic of Germany remain in the text, with explanatory language in brackets, where appropriate. —Walter Zettl & Jane Seigler

Foreword

Every professional organization has its own professional ethical standards. These are characterized by the technical abilities and special training of its members, as well as by their moral conduct. Once the notion of correct work or the commitment to quality and value given is discarded, the professional group next forfeits the respect of the world, then its professional standing, and finally its entire raison d'être is drawn into question. Above all, young professional riders will meet, upon completing their period of training, an increasing number of good amateur riders and ever greater demands with regard to the sport. In order that they, like their predecessors of the past, may in future be considered the very backbone of horsemanship, their further education immediately following their professional examinations must be logical and consistent. Only in this way can passion and joy in their profession be sustained.

This small booklet consciously avoids any pretentious creative story-telling. Neither is it a prescription for how to ride or how to teach riding. It is rather intended to remind the professional trainer of his responsibilities to his horses and his students, and to make clear the values of the profession. It goes without saying that the repeated use of the designation, "professional rider," "professional trainer," and "riding instructor," as well as the use of the pronouns "he" and "his," applies also to the female representatives of our profession.

Guenther Festerling
Griesstadt, Spring 1997

1. The Significance of the Horseman's Professional Standing

The professional horseman preserves the classical manner of riding and thereby upholds the standards for contemporary riding. Ever more urgent is his mission to arrest today's progressive divergence from the recognized principles of horsemanship, and regularly to put to proof their correctness and absolute necessity. The highest levels of performance can only be attained when preeminent practicing trainers instill thorough, technically skilled training in riders and horses at the basic and intermediate levels. A top performance can only be built on well-ridden, complete basics. Mastery of the various levels of this discipline can not, however, be the only mission of the professional horseman. It is proper to set new and worthy standards of horsemanship, in order to fulfill an educational mission to the riding public, and to make it relevant to today's riders. Conscientious, cultivated riding should guide us back to increased self-discipline, patience, and regard for this creature, the horse. In lieu of the pursuit of success at any price, we should place a higher priority on the pleasure of producing a genuinely well-trained and correctly moving horse.

The qualities of a truly well-ridden, all-around horse must once again become a goal worthy of striving after. If we do not reach this goal, more and more recreational riders will switch to other, so-called "easier" riding disciplines, opting understandably to ride an increasing number of non-domestically bred horses. Such a development can not be in the best interests of the domestic horse breeding industry.

2. The Equestrian Mission of the Professional Horseman

Only a rider who has undergone a lengthy tuition in
self-discipline and patience is worthy of the name.

This mission is multi-faceted and highly exacting. It is disastrous to believe that the skillful training of horses is required only for the lofty demands of good riders. The basic education of the horse, his further training as an all-around useful animal, and especially his correction in all areas requires more than average ability on the part of the rider, although not necessarily equal to the abilities of a top-ranked trainer. Riders with only moderate practical skills in the saddle will not be able to meet these demands.

The Training of the Young Horse

It is the absolute duty of the professional horseman to provide the horse with a very painstaking, and above all a carefully planned basic education. This phase is to be regarded as laying the foundational prerequisites for any continued training of the horse, and can be decisive with regard to his later assured existence. Here, errors and omissions can have painful consequences, causing even a young horse at the beginning of his career to require constant correction, or even to become a 'rogue.'

One needs to pay special attention during this portion of the formative development of the versatile horse, to the creation and preservation of an implicit, unlimited trust between horse and rider, and to guaranteeing the carrying ability of the horse's back with a view to ensuring he will be able to carry greater weight later on, as he achieves more complete *Losgelassenheit*.

The Further Development of the Horse

In further developing the horse, one must also strive for a systematic, increasing, gymnasticizing of horses of all riding disciplines, through more bending work, development of thrusting power and movement, and more complete *Durchlässigkeit* and corresponding collection. In order to do this, the rider must establish a carefully considered training plan that addresses the horse's physical condition, his potential, his temperament and his learning ability, while shunning any excessive demands.

The calling cards of the good professional are obedient, happy horses with completely unconstrained, rhythmic, coiled-spring-like ways of going, who are calm and trustworthy at home and out in the countryside, showing a marked interest in their work. Boring, repetitious work is to be avoided at all costs with horses who, at this stage of their development, demonstrate a recognizable talent for a specific equestrian discipline. Such work will spoil the horse's pleasure in the tasks set for him, and will discourage his willingness to perform. In any case, this would reduce the assessed value of an expensive horse, and will do no honor to his trainer.

The Training of the Useful Horse

In addition to naturally talented horses, horses with limited abilities are also entitled to a solid training regimen. No conscientious, horse-loving trainer who takes to heart the future of the horses entrusted to him will allow them to come to harm through the neglect caused by not providing such a regimen. Such a horse will surely find a good home (by human calculations) if, through improved suitability in conjunction with obedience, it becomes a desirable partner for lower-level competition, and, eventually, develops into a horse that can be used for a variety of purposes or as a reliable recreational riding horse.

Retraining Badly-Ridden or Spoiled Horses

Successful retraining of a badly-moving or even a ruined horse is frequently his last chance. Every professional horseman should be aware of that. Understandably, no one wants to ride poor movers that are uncomfortable to sit, and such horses are therefore often to be discarded. This is reason enough for the enthusiastic professional, when the occasion arises, to take on such horses with calm patience, and, with appropriate empathy, to turn them into useful "members of society." Anyone who sets himself this difficult task must believe in the eventual success of his efforts, keeping in mind the equestrian precept, "No horse can evade the effect of the correct influence of the rider." The necessary patience and long hours are quite often nobly rewarded.

The Development of Highly Talented Horses

It is understandably the dream of every professional horseman to train highly gifted horses for the demands of the FEI levels, and perhaps to exhibit them personally at elite competitions. The most important precept here is to correctly assess each individual horse's potential, and to avoid asking too much of him. This temptation has defeated even experienced riders, because such horses often offer everything so early, and their great potential for ridability seduces their riders into first accepting, and then forcefully demanding, these offers. Here we see the validity of another old precept: "Take it easy, and take your time." A horse that is being developed for the purpose of being used as a sport horse absolutely must be thoroughly gymnasticized and highly motivated. To achieve both these ends at the same time requires great skill on the part of the rider, in conjunction with a personality that is highly empathetic and tactful.

The Participation of Professional Horsemen in the Competitive Arena

Whether a professional trainer is able to take part in classes at the FEI levels depends on his own skills and abilities as well as the quality of the horses at his disposal. No matter how difficult the test, this public test of the rider's abilities is nevertheless to be regarded as absolutely necessary.

Participation in horse shows should regularly renew the professional horseman's motivation for his daily work. He who rides only in his own quiet little ring will at some point lose his enthusiasm for work, and also the heart for any bold adventure in the saddle. Therefore, beyond the opportunity that showing offers to check the quality of his own work and his horse's ridability, the professional horseman can also gain understanding and motivation for further work.

The horses he presents for competition are the "business cards" that reveal the pro's technical ability and his riding artistry. The horses he shows must be more than equal to the demands of the current test, and even in the warm-up ring should show convincing proof of solid preparation. After a disappointing presentation, subsequent work must be appropriate, to the point, and temperate, and may never under any circumstances degenerate into roughness.

The Significance of Theoretical Knowledge

Every trainer who is interested in his specialty will want to know what others who have gone before him in the saddle have felt and discovered. All theories come from practice and should, in turn, be of benefit in practical application. A good foundation of theoretical knowledge is an indispensable supplement to practical skill. It must be so deeply absorbed that all the precepts of the man-horse relationship are anchored fast in the pro's consciousness, to save him from spontaneous errors in his hands-on work, and to serve as the basis for teaching that keeps these principles in mind.

The Obligation of the Rider to Further His Own Development

Learn theory, or you'll always be a bungler!

The professional trainer often rides alone, without supervision or technical advice. Under these circumstances, despite all his vigilance and self discipline, errors often creep into the work with more difficult horses to the detriment of their further development. Therefore, even experienced professional horsemen should afford themselves the opportunity to be corrected and advised by competent colleagues. Such persons will furnish genuinely helpful assistance only when they are themselves occupied in the successful practice of training horses, and do not enjoy only theoretical information.

Young professionals who have finished their apprenticeships begin their further education immediately. The skills and knowledge from their education to date, though hard-earned, are by no means sufficient to make a living as a professional horseman.

For the next two to three years, the young professional should pursue self-supporting work in dressage, jumping, and three-day eventing, respectively, as well as in his field of specialization, under the supervision of competent teachers, and so prepare himself for the practical requirements of his Professional Instructor's examination. Beyond this exam, such a significant investment of time will prove to be the best guarantor of a future career as a successful upper-level professional rider, instructor, trainer, or coach. Use should also be made of refresher courses and clinics of all kinds.

A well-rounded advanced education is also necessary because only the synergy of the aids learned through experience in all the riding disciplines will make it possible to be effective in any specialty later decide upon.

3. The Teaching Mission of the Professional Horseman

The best system of instruction in the world is meaningless,
if it isn't converted into practice by suitable instructors.

The absolute prerequisite for the successful fulfillment of the teaching mission of the professional horseman is his own equestrian skill. The contention that less able riders can be excellent teachers is a myth. Only solid, demonstrated, practical skill in all areas, and the experience won therefrom, will enable him to pass along the exacting requirements in his instruction to others in any field of endeavor.

The example of his personal attitude and behavior towards the horse earns him the respect and attention of his students, and is not to be replaced by even the greatest pedagogical ability. A young person who is interested in riding as a sport needs equestrian models, not theoreticians.

Moreover, no teaching mission can be fulfilled exclusively from the ground. Oftentimes the instructor must ride a horse in a fashion that will facilitate the student's catching on to the right feeling, or in order to undertake a necessary correction. It is far from sufficient merely to be able to explain to a student what he should do or should let happen.

The teaching mission of the professional horseman begins effectively during his *Bereitertätigkeit* [time as a professional rider, before receiving his professional teacher's license]. Here a significant complement to his own work will be the effectiveness of his teaching the owner of the horses that are entrusted to him for training.

Principles of Instruction

Exacting teaching does not begin first at the advanced levels. A thorough education in the basics is the essential prerequisite for the successful further development of the riding student, as well as for the horse.

When teaching beginners, one must emphasize supple and flexible following of the movement of the horse, in addition to the development of a correct position. Advanced riders should take advantage of any opportunity to work on the development of the seat.

The objective of more advanced work is the precise use and smooth coordination of the aids and the development of the rider's sense of "feel." In jumping, riders should practice and master a light seat and the security of the seat over the jump, as well as a sensitive and rhythmic canter between the fences.

These concepts, in connection with a freely carried, flexible hand, are the cornerstones of equestrian development. One must constantly monitor them and assure their preservation, in order to have a good base for future training accomplishments.

The increased effectiveness of the advanced pupil will enable him to systematically gymnasticize his horse, and will give the riding teacher opportunity to make his training activity ever more interesting and effective.

Characteristics and Functions of the Professional Riding Instructor

Of greatest importance is the need to pass along to his students his own ability and knowledge, not just to seek his own success in the saddle. In addition to an unrestricted readiness to teach, the riding teacher must also find joy in the successful experiences of others. Teaching is not a part-time job, but in the majority of cases is the primary mission of the professional riding instructor.

Besides the pedagogical knowledge he has acquired through a logical and concentrated progression, the instructor must also possess the ability to treat all his students with understanding and marked good will. The more he recognizes his own equestrian problems, the easier this will be for him. He must always be able to motivate anew students of any age, and possess a pronounced sensitivity to their potential and to their mental state. The regular structure of his hours of instruction, technically correct and meaningful corrections, as well as his quality of radiating confidence as a teacher, will help students over uncertainties and setbacks and to teach them to formulate their own realistic and appropriate goals.

The instructor must complement his practical teaching with transmission of a thorough understanding of theoretical knowledge, so that his pupils can recognize and put to practical use all of the concepts of classical horsemanship.

One of the major tasks of the professional riding instructor is to inculcate all the worthwhile concepts of complete horsemanship in riding and handling the horse. He is to train up young riders in particular to exhibit attentiveness and discipline, and further develop their sensitivity to the horse.

The teacher is also responsible for his students away from his own stables. After careful preparation for their public appearance at horse shows, he is responsible for their correct behavior in the warm-up areas as well as in the dressage ring, the stadium, or the cross-country course. Riders he has chosen to bring along should always exhibit impeccable sportsmanlike conduct. Unfriendly behavior towards fellow competitors should be as unacceptable to the teacher as uncomplimentary remarks about other horses, and particularly about judges and stewards. Bringing riders up to be good sports and to embody the behavior expected of a true horseman must be a main objective of the professional instructor. These qualities are also prerequisites for successful further training and for the preservation of an honorable sport.

A passionate riding teacher always should have an open ear for the problems of riders of other riding disciplines in his area and, within the scope of his knowledge and ability, stand by them in word and deed. In the final analysis, they are all horse people, and presumption and disinterest are anathema to a genuine horseman. Only he who has acquired the attention and trust of his students has found the right path to successful training!

4. The Cruelty-Prevention Mission of the Professional Horseman

Being a rider also means always putting the welfare of the horse first.

Here, too, the professional horseman's personal example in the saddle is of primary importance. No horse can extricate itself from being put into service by humans. Beginning with the first day under saddle, the horse must bear humans on its back for the remainder of its life. This fact alone is reason enough for each rider to conduct his work with the horse in such a way as not to damage it physically or mentally, and beyond that, so that it maintains its well-being.

If the latter is not the case, any conception of harmony between human and animal becomes a lying farce. No serious rider who calls his horse his partner may become its slavemaster.

The professional horseman in particular must oppose any unprofessional rough treatment of the horse, not only in public, but also when working at home. He should never forget that he is the representative of a system of riding that makes no provision for force. The effectiveness of his aids in the saddle must be so great that, through their intensified effect and calm consequence, he can overcome any difficulty and counter any recalcitrance displayed by his horse.

When punishment is appropriate, it must be measured and moderate, and may never arise out of intemperate and excessive rage. Anyone who has made a habit of rough riding and does not rigorously turn away from it, renders his abilities ridiculous. He will also be responsible if his students adopt the brutal practices of their bad role-model, and thereby offend in an extraordinary way the honor of his profession.

Only his own irreproachable behavior can put the professional horseman into a position to prevent the rough and unfeeling behavior of his students, without respect to station. Eventually, any apparent disadvantage generated by such impeccable conduct will be outweighed by the trustworthiness won in such a way. It is his function to facilitate "horsemanship." The salient feature of this concept, however, is the maintenance of an attitude of fairness towards the horse when one's own desires and dreams are not fulfilled. If riders who are otherwise inclined shun the influence and control of the professional horseman, it would be better if he cut himself off from them, rather than to allow himself to be identified with them.

The health and welfare of the horse have priority over everything else. Adequate and ever-improving knowledge of veterinary science should enable the professional horseman to constantly and conscientiously oversee the well-being of the horses entrusted to his care, and to provide first aid in the case of any emergency. Training objectives must be postponed whenever the condition of the horse is less than desirable, as must any intended participation in competition.

It goes without saying that the professional horseman must consistently refuse any manipulation of the horse through medication or unauthorized devices; this is a question of honor! Further animal protection functions of the professional include cultivating well-founded knowledge of all other requirements of the horse, such as correct movement, proper shoeing, correct feeding and modern stable management.

5. Moral Obligations of the Professional Horseman

There is nothing objectionable about earning money by training horses and riders, as long as it doesn't lead to unsound practice with regard to humans and animals. Earning money is good. Earning money while keeping one's good name is better. Earning good money while keeping one's good name is the best. The honest professional who cares about maintaining the trust of his clientele must adhere scrupulously to clear and unequivocally worded contracts that spell out the particular activities that are expected in exchange for a given sum of money.

Absolute reliability is an indispensable prerequisite for professional success as a horseman. This reliability must extend to all areas of his activity. Students of all ages and stages of accomplishment must be assured that their education is conscientiously undertaken and of the greatest possible trustworthiness. Those who trust a professional with the training of their horses must be able to rely on their being properly and honorably ridden, and further, that their reasonable needs will be provided for.

How many horses the professional can take for training will always depend on the particular circumstances of his work situation, as well as the number and quality of his assistants. In any case, he must guarantee that he does not take on more horses than he has time to cope with. The professional must also be enough of a horseman that he will not allow himself to undertake premature and incorrect training procedures because of the false expectations of a horse's owner.

When acting as a sales agent, the professional must also attach importance to the concept that any horse he recommends must be a suitable match for the equestrian ability, as well as the desires and expectations, of the buyer. Any appropriate commission to which he may be entitled as agent ought never to become the primary consideration. Anyone who acts as agent for a horse and recommends its purchase also bears responsibility for his advice.

No professional rider should, in his own interest or in the interest of his profession, express deprecatory remarks about colleagues or pass negative judgements about other horses and riders. Those who find it necessary to do so are themselves not worth much, as a rule.

It is in the best interest of the horse, and of the Sport itself, to consciously disassociate oneself from colleagues who, through unsportsmanlike and dishonorable behavior, bring into disrepute the ethical standards of the profession.

The professional trainer ought never to forget that he is a role model, a function never to be undervalued, especially for young would-be horsemen. Appropriate clothing, cleanliness, punctuality, accessibility, and above all a respectful impression with regard to the opposite sex in word, conduct, and behavior - all these will never give rise to doubts about his moral integrity.

6. Educating The Next Generation of Professional Horsemen

A profession will be only worth as much as its next generation expects.

Every professional riding instructor who is in a position to educate the next generation of professionals should make the most of this opportunity. The education of a prospective professional must be so goal-oriented and intensively undertaken in the short time available, having as its objective not only the passing of the professional certification examinations, but also furnishing the student with a well-grounded foundation for his later professional activity.

At the beginning of the apprenticeship period, the master teacher has to function as a professional advisor or counselor. It would be irresponsible of him to permit young people to imagine their "dream profession" without frankly explaining to them the risks, conditions, and demands of the profession they have chosen. During the probationary period it must be determined whether the apprentice has any talent as a horseman, as well as whether he exhibits a steadfast character, readiness to perform, perseverance, and will power. Extraordinary weight should be placed on a friendly and open nature.

Only when these and similar prerequisites are evident should the prospective professional's education be continued after the probationary period. Otherwise at the end there will be three losers: the master teacher, the student, and the entire profession.

A basically sound education in all areas of service to horses is indispensable for later professional success. Starting with the very first day, the apprentice must feel that he is a part of the operation, and should be entrusted with clearly outlined tasks. Relevant and friendly instruction is just as important for him as the feeling that the boss worries about him and is always available to talk to him. The greatest importance is to be attached to the reliable and conscientious completion of all tasks assigned to the apprentice.

The apprentice's education in horsemanship should also begin at this time, of which by far the greater part should take place under supervision and guidance. The apprentice must always have horses available which are appropriate to his level of accomplishment, and ought to ride young horses with the same increasing adeptness as he does older horses who have progressed further in their training. Dressage, jumping and cross-country riding must be taught equally.

Particularly in the second half of the apprenticeship, riding in the double bridle and stadium jumping should not be neglected; neither should the apprentice neglect to begin and constantly improve his ability to instruct beginners and advanced riders.

Occasional participation in the competitive arena can help the apprentice build confidence about the impending exams, and to gain more experience in competitive situations.

Because the apprentice must put himself to the proof by riding a Level L test [2nd Level equivalent] for his professional certification, one could actually expect that he will by this point in time already have fulfilled the requirements at Level M [3rd Level equivalent].

Careful monitoring of the apprentice's notebooks will serve as an examination of his theoretical knowledge. By eliciting theoretical knowledge from the apprentice during practical riding sessions, the master teacher helps the apprentice to apply this theory in practice, and to instill these connections in his consciousness.

Tutelage in politeness, willingness to oblige, and helpfulness to his colleagues and others in his field will complete the apprentice's education and allow him to become an esteemed coworker even while he is still in training.

A curriculum arranged in such a manner will, on the one hand, enable the apprentice to successfully complete his final examinations, and on the other, will send him on his way with the appropriate and necessary self-confidence and make him reliable in his later professional activities.

The professional horseman may constantly take joy in his activities when he is equipped through skill and knowledge to conduct himself impeccably under all conditions in a difficult profession. These qualities will also help him to avoid being manipulated.

judges are the guardians of the art of riding

interview with Christophe Hess, from *Reiter-Revue* translation by Lynne Sprinsky

Short necks, tension in place of expression—the judge is supposed to pull the emergency brake on the erroneous development of training. **Reiter-Revue** *editor Patricia Titje spoke with leading FN trainer and Grand Prix judge Christoph Hess about the duties, responsibilities, and future of his guild.*

RR: The winner is supposed to be viewed by everyone as a winner, really. But often we end up with differing assessments on the part of the public, the judge, the rider.

Hess: Opinions differ not only among riders and the public, but even among the judges themselves. Sometimes the varying locations of the judges can explain the differences. But large discrepancies can arise in the rating of a single horse for the same movement. Klaus Balkenhol's Goldstern was an example. From the short end of the arena he got sevens or eights for the half-pass, but from the long side he often got only a six. From that location, the lateral gaits weren't correctly balanced.

RR: Often it's less about a point's difference in a single movement than about the basic quality of what one is offered in the arena.

Hess: Judges are the guardians of the art of riding. They have to assess whether the rider and horse are on the right, the classical, path, or whether it's all about clever cheating that the horse isn't truly on the aids and doesn't go correctly with active hind legs over the back nor through the neck. Consideration of the training scale must always run through the marks like a red thread, and can't first come into play in the Collective Marks, which explicitly ask about the activity of the mouth, submission and *durchlässigkeit* (throughness). Persistent deficiencies today include the often-absent *Losgelassenheit* (relaxation) and incorrect contact. I would suggest to my judge-colleagues that they use up the whole range of marks at separate proceedings. Give a very good performance a nine or a ten, and rate the weak or faulty movement correspond-ingly negatively. Giving only fives, sixes or sevens helps neither the riders nor the trainers, and the spectators least of all.

RR: Many riders wish there were more practitioners at the judge's tables.

Hess: Different models of accreditation could simplify becoming a judge for suc-cessful riders and trainers. But a good rider is not automatically also a dedicated judge. I know that my profile as a rider is limited. When I was still active as a rider, I dreamed of riding Grand Prix on a horse I'd trained entirely by myself. But you have to know your limitations, too. So I have put a lot of motivation and passion for this sport into my judge's position. And even without having ridden Grand Prix success-fully, I know how I need to rate what I see in the tests.

RR: With their list of placings, judges reward the results of the training that hap-pens at home. But even this training, in part, is being fiercely discussed.

Hess: The judge only sees the horse for seven minutes. Riders like Anky van Grunsven grant glimpses into their daily training and set themselves apart with criti-cism of their methods. With other riders, no one knows how they work their horses at home. But from the first halt/salute, we still have to decide whether this horse and its training correspond to the textbook. Here the walk is a wonderful example. A tense horse that's being held will not produce strides that are rhythmically regular. Because what a lot of amateurs do at home doesn't necessarily conform to the FN guidelines. Speaking of which, particular horses, sure, can require special methods. Not force or coercion, but other ways of training. For example, what Anky van Grunsven practices should not simply be adopted wholesale. With some riders it often seems not to be the goal to get a horse relaxed, but rather to cultivate tension. But whether I like a partic-ular "training method" or not can't play any role when I judge. Here I must only judge what I see in the arena. If a horse isn't securely in front of the driving aids, or doesn't swing its back in the trot, I can take that into consideration in the marks I assign. It's the same with a contact that's permanently enforced with the hand. The back is gen-erally blocked and the riders can't sit it. Further signs of a lack of relaxation are con-stant switching of the tail, and also the look on the horse's face and the play of its ears will give away a lot. Here the judge has to really focus his attention; then he can justi-fy a poor mark from time to time. Just looking for an active hind leg is definitely not enough, because a strong rider can force even that.

RR: So how could more influence be exerted, from official quarters, on correct training at home?

Hess: What's practiced at home is what's required at the competition. So there should be more tests given that assess the rider's capabilities. A step in the right direc-tion was the development of the Dressage Equitation test. But those need to be adver-tised much more often by the competition organizers. Because when a rider doesn't take pains with his seat and its correct effect, then pretty soon riding has an air of ani-mal abuse about it.

The difficulty began some time ago. In the arena, I can only adhere to the rating scale and give comments. But it would be equally important to supervise the warm-up. In the warm-up ring, not only must warnings about the use of spurs and whips be given, but also psychic terror. Here, the supervising judge, or for international competitions, the stewards must step in. A horse that's being gagged on its chest the whole time can't really relax itself. Warming-up like that is not compatible with ethical principles.

RR: Why do so few judges have the courage to really evaluate what they see?

Hess: The basic maxims should first be benevolently positive. If necessary, the right things must be stressed even with the big names. But don't underestimate the pressure on the judges. There's a big lobby that is frequently heard from. In order to created a unified and correct way of judging, I could imagine a permanent kind of supervision for judges like that for psychologists. The supervisor (observer) should help find solutions to problems that arise during the judging process. That doesn't mean that in the end everyone will think alike, but one could differ within the context of a conversation about the rating criteria as regards specific riders or presentations.

the complete picture of the properly ridden horse

by Col. von Heydebreck
translation by Paul Schopf and Jane Seigler

Col. Hans von Heydebreck (1866-1935) is one of the organizers for the German **Reitvorschrift** *(Rule Book) in 1912, based on the work of Steinbrecht (1808-1885). This book was written for the army and still forms the basics of the current rule book.*

The overall picture of the well-ridden horse can be summarized in the following manner:

Sure and light, the horse's feet lift off and return to the ground in a clear and correct beat that results from a lively self propulsion without any unsteadiness or rushing. He moves through the figures without force, effortlessly executing the rider's wishes. The horse's neck arches evenly upwards in front of the rider. His head, softly giving at the poll, is positioned so that the nose is just in front of the vertical. The ears are the highest point without pointing forward or laying back. Instead, their natural relaxed carriage indicates to the observer the horse's willingness and attentiveness towards its rider. The horse's eye focuses confidently on its path of travel. The mouth is closed, and light foaming indicates that the horse is chewing the bit softly, without making any grinding noises.

The reins form a steady and even contact with the horse's mouth without hanging loose. One sees elasticity of the curb rein, which allows the horse to step confidently forward to the bit, maintaining correct contact on both reins. When the rider gives briefly with the hand [ed: *Überstreichen*], the horse's position, rhythm and gait do not change. This shows that the horse carries itself and is not expecting to be supported by the rider's hand. Should the rider decide to give more or lengthen the reins further, the horse will stretch its head and neck confidently forward without pulling downward or throwing its head upwards. The horse searches for an even contact on the reins. An imperceptible soft closing of the hand will result in a downward transition of the gait or a complete halt, in which the horse remains standing in a proud posture, square, motionless, and evenly balanced on all four legs. The slightest pressure of the rider's calves takes the horse immediately and without any hesitation into the requested gait.

All movements occur without any force and seem to originate from the elastically swinging back of the horse. The quiet and pleasant seat of the rider testifies to how comfortable he feels on the horse and how well the horse moves. Throughout, everything remains in *Schwung*. Every step and every stride comes from the willing, ready flexion of the upper joints and very powerful lifting of the hind legs, which either push the horse's body steadily forward or give it more support, depending on the degree of collection and strength within the gait. The hind legs must still support and lighten the forehand during more extended gaits. On the other hand, during collected movements, the pushing power is transformed through stronger bending of the joints into carrying power but the steps must remain animated. This enables the forehand to lift easily away from the ground. Then, the rider may allow the shoulder more freedom, thereby giving the horse room to move more forward. Or, the rider may limit the forward movement of the shoulder. The forearm will then come almost horizontal, lifting the forehand and the horse's steps will become more elevated appearing hardly to touch the ground.

When viewed from the side, one has the impression that the rider is sitting in the middle of the horse, half of the horse in front and half behind. From the ears to the lightly swinging and loosely carried tail goes a smoothly undulating line without any sharp angles. The withers stay a little higher than the highest point of the croup.

Viewed from the front, the hind legs should never lose the track of the front legs, except in the lateral work. The head of the horse stays vertical so both ears are level. The neck extends straight forward from the body of the horse. When ridden with flexion one sees the inside of the forehead, the inside shoulder and the inside hip almost in one line. The shoulders of the rider extend out evenly on both sides of the neck; his head appears between the ears of the horse. Horse and rider are molded almost into one. They create a very fine, balanced unit—a living sculpture. The pleasing form and gracefulness coupled with clockwork precision and regular but powerful movement make the picture complete.

classical dressage verus 'competitive dressage'

by Doris K. Halstead

The body tells all. It is not necessary to see the performance to know whether a horse has been trained in the true classical manner or for the competitive market.

Competitive dressage of course should be no different from classical. However, in this modern age we tend to rush everything. Racing horses must race at 2, cutting horses must win futurities for 2 year olds, dressage horses must be in training classes at 2 and on and on. What is this doing to our horses, our partners? Classically trained compatriots of these "child pawns" are not started under saddle till they are 3 or 4 years old.

Initial training is the primary differentiation between classical and 'competitive'. In part, the problem arises when the training is rushed and in part from a total misunderstanding of, or not caring how, to properly assist the horse in attaining 'self carriage'. It is much faster (in the early stages) to hold the horse in a 'frame' then push him into the bridle. After that all movements are taught by blocking the unwanted movements so the horse learns to shut down. This, I believe, is the primary reason for nearly all the physical problems of the 'competitively' trained horse. The horse will lean into the bridle, becoming heavier and heavier in the hand or tuck behind the bridle. Either of these evasions will result in improper muscle development and discomfort. Hence, the possibility of finding balance is lost.

Competitive dressage and other training has just gotten more aggressive in the new "rollkur" or "riding deep" techniques. Long work periods in this extreme position cause the neck to develop a double "breakover" so they have a serious "broken neck" look as well as being consistently over flexed at the poll. There are further consequences as well.

Any time a group of muscles is forced to be used in an overly shortened position, they are most likely to go into spasm. Try, while standing, holding one foot close to your buttocks with your hand. Then make a concerted effort to hold it there with your knee flexor muscles and let go with your hand. You will immediately get a spasm in those muscles. This is what is being done to the horse that is forced to maintain an unnatural position for a period of time. The period of time to cause the spasm varies a great deal from person to person and horse to horse but it consistently occurs. I have seen horses tied nose to tail (supposedly to correct lack of lateral bend) go into spasm, fall down and NEVER recover from the muscle injuries that occur when this happens. It appears that horses that are ridden in the "rollkur" have the same problem, in that, the neck does not recover and forever has a "broken" appearance. Yes, the abdominal muscles are exercised a great deal more but this is accomplished at the expense of the back muscles that become overly stretched and unable to correctly contract, when the head is brought into elevation, to protect the back from dropping and therefore from injury. Just look at many humans that have overstretched back muscles and ligaments. They stand with forward head and shoulders and even though they would want to stand erect, it is impossible. Though they may be able to come to the erect position, they automatically fall back to the slouch whenever a thought or movement takes their concentration away.

Would we expect our horses to do more than we humans are able? Once we and horses alike, are stretched to this asymmetry, we are unable to function in good alignment. Our strength and automatic choice of position for function always lies in the range of movement that is most familiar and somewhere between easily available ranges.

That translates as follows. The horse needs to be worked where he is in self carriage, gently coaxing him to push into the bridle while coaxing him to the desired elevation as he can handle it. That is, not over flexed anywhere in the neck and at a level he can participate without getting a spasm. When the desired position is attained by coaxing a higher level of elevation as he is able and allowing rests (including long and low but not over flexed at the poll), he will develop in all ranges giving flexibility and fluidity of movement. This allows the horse to strengthen gradually assuring he will continue to be able to progress. Asking too much too soon will "lock" the muscles and progress will stop. Continuous work in any forced position will confirm that motor pattern. Therefore, the horse will find other evasions to keep that forced pattern when asked to do additional movement patterns. Having made the point re the physical problems that result from this training, they are a drop in the bucket compared to what you have lost in terms of your horse's trust and gained in problems of stress.

One look at a horse's outline will tell whether or not the training is classical or competitive. Classical training will assure that the muscles of the top line are well developed and flexible. The abdominal muscles are well developed and in harmony with the back that is fluid and lifted in self carriage, as seen in figure 1.

The overall look is of smooth undulating connection, front to back with withers higher than the croup. This comes when the rider has taken the time and effort to learn how to "talk" to the horse through the seat and legs and use the bridle only for conversation involving left right balance and what level of self carriage is expected, expecting only that level the horse can do without causing spasm and pain. Then the

The horse's top line and skeletal position in classical self-carriage. The rider is carried elevated. The poll is the highest point. The head is carried between 80 and 90 degrees of flexion.

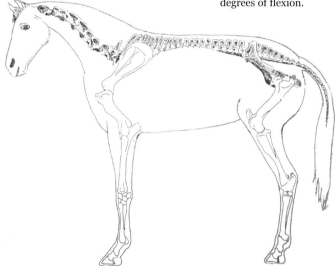

Figure 1

way is left open for the horse to move forward freely. A classically trained horse becomes more and more beautiful as his training progresses.

Alois Podhajsky loved to tell the story about a carriage horse he was training, a mare he loved because she was so attentive and had an excellent temperament. A superior officer told him he should not bother with that ugly mare as she was far too ugly to ever win any prizes. A few years later the officer saw him perform and came to tell him that he was glad to see he had taken his advice and gotten a much more beautiful animal. It was the same mare with just a couple years good classical training "under her belt."

Competitively trained horses have over stretched and painful muscles at the poll and in the back. There will be muscles in spasm and in pain at the throatlatch, base of the neck, and possibly the abdominals. Suspensory ligament injuries and hock and stifle problems are common. As training progresses, the horse loses his natural gaits and movement becomes less fluid. The withers drop and the horse appears downhill even though conformation would indicate he should not be. The tips of the thoracic vertebra approximate and become sensitive. All this happens because the horse was not allowed to move freely into the bridle. "Competitive training is like cramming your camping gear in a stuff sack. It gets wrinkled and if you cram too much it breaks. Thus horses "shut down" or become sour or unruly.

The "rollkur" training works the horse nearly exclusively in excess neck flexion as shown in figure 2.

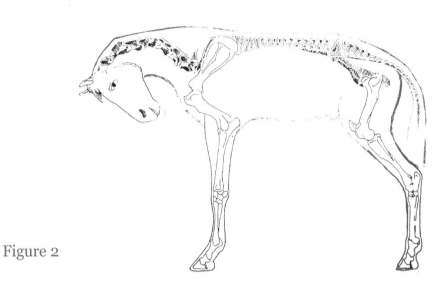

Figure 2

Picture the muscles of the underside of the neck being in extreme shortened position, which encourages the neck flexors to hypertrophy and shorten. Muscles thicken under the jaw making ease of breathing difficult. The scalenii muscles at the bottom of the neck will also shorten making the neck inverted. Note the dropped withers, (also shown in figure 4B). Muscles of the back are overstretched, developing them in the elongated position, making it impossible for them to shorten properly for back support when the head/neck is elevated. When head/neck elevation is requested the only way to get it is to compact the neck, hollow the back, leave the withers dropped, and trail behind. You have now created a horse that is working in abnormal movement patterns, has loss of fluid movement, is in pain and is feeling seriously stressed.

Both holding a frame and forcing the horse into the bridle and the "rollkur" techniques will result in a horse that develops as the one shown in figure 3, though the "rollkur" trained horse is more likely to have a broken neck appearance.

When I have clients at a barn where classical training is the "modus operandi" the problems I see are related to having slipped in the pasture or having caught a hip on a doorway.

Please note the two horses in figure 1 and 4A compared to figure 3 and 4B. The classically trained horse appears to be taller, have better proportions and to have a longer neck. These figures were constructed from the exact same skeleton. Shoulder girdle muscles of the classically trained horse carry the torso elevated between the shoulder blades. The "competitively" trained horse tends to allow the torso to be carried low between the shoulder blades. Classically trained horses often measure significantly taller as they have developed their musculature with training. As you can see,

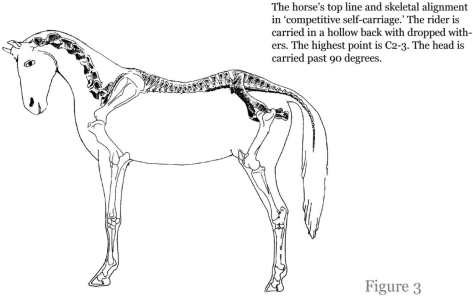

The horse's top line and skeletal alignment in 'competitive self-carriage.' The rider is carried in a hollow back with dropped withers. The highest point is C2-3. The head is carried past 90 degrees.

Figure 3

Form follows function: compare figures 1 through 4B.

Classical carriage. This high withers carriage allows the horse to lower his torso in readiness to spring up for those lofty gaits we love so.

'Competitive' carriage. This low slung carriage of the torso does not allow for the springiness of gaits and leads to over stretch of the pectorals and bunching of the trapezius and other muscles of the withers.

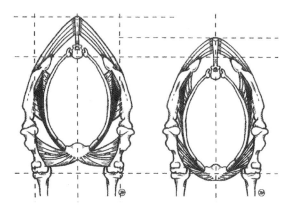

Figure 4A   Figure 4B

some muscles become over stretched and others over shortened in the dropped torso scenario. Properly trained horses become significantly more beautiful and better proportioned as their correct training progresses. Proper head/neck carriage reveals the horse's true length of neck.

In addition to the before mentioned problems, "competitively" trained horses are pushed for more strength and submissiveness than their muscles and psyche are able to tolerate. They become fearful, sour and disobedient. They get stuck at level 1, 2, or 3, as they have too many restrictions to be able to do the upper level work. Saddle fit is a constant problem as they have improperly developed muscles around the withers and the muscles fluctuate with the improper training. Many problems such as tongue carried too high or sticking out, mouth open, tossing the head, fearfulness, shying, quickness or aggressiveness develop. Many of the problems are very difficult if impossible to reverse and in any event take longer to correct than they did to create.

Watching the world championships and some of the qualifiers in person was a real treat but also an eye opener. Many of the riders were really pushing to get the perfect performance. The horses were under such stresses and being pushed so hard it was not surprising to see many who were off in their gaits, unruly, or just unable to perform. I saw one back out of the ring after halt at X. I saw another who needed to be packed in ice after his performance the expectation of his muscle inflammation was so great. Excessively pushing the horse, even for the last minute preps for a show, loses his trust in the rider and in the hand of the rider, especially at show time.

Classical dressage builds the horse slowly but steadily. This way the horse can develop without being over faced and physical and emotional problems are avoided. The three gaits are kept pure and are enhanced as the strength and endurance progresses naturally. When horses are treated with this respect they become our partner and the performance is greatly improved as it becomes a cooperative effort. This kind of training needs lots of self discipline from the rider. Often the horse has responded to a request the rider has given inadvertently. If the rider is being truly attentive he will realize the horse was right. Punishment for responses to our subtle and inadvertent aids, because the rider does not know any better will result in horses shutting down to our aids. The horse knows where we are looking and what we are thinking almost before we do. He knows if we are stiff in any areas and will tend to image hisself after that stiffness. He also knows where we are weak and will mimic that as well. When he is not punished for these talents, he will come to react to the slightest and almost invisible aids and bring all his strength and beauty to our beck and call.

Many riders are unable to be calm enough in their own psyche to hear and feel how the horse is responding. Maintaining a calm and clear influence, progressing gently and smoothly, avoiding things that give the horse stress or fear will result in the horse giving his all in strength and beauty to our slightest and nearly invisible aids.

Many feel this is the long path to the upper levels but not having any setbacks is the surest and shortest way to the goal.

Training snafus are hard to correct once established. Many people with time and caring have obtained excellent horses that have been incorrectly trained and have come to a block in their training. They must take the horse back to ground zero and establish self carriage taking extra care to not progress too rapidly. Even then if the horse gets into a perceived stress situation all his "phobias" will come to surface and his incorrect responses will come to light. It is best to progress with the young untrained horse gradually bolstering his self confidence as you go. A great trainer once said, "Set it up so he cannot fail, then praise him for what he does".

Although there are other forms of problems from the competitive rather than classical approaches to dressage, the following table lists common accurate comparisons.

Competitive Dressage	**Classical Dressage**
False collection, results in:	True collection results in:
Weak back, stretched abs	Strong back/abdominal synergy
Spasm at base of neck	Developed topline poll to tail
Back spasm	Well developed back muscles
Stuck at 2nd or 3rd level	Progresses steadily but slowly
Poll flexed past 90 degrees	Poll flexed from 80 to 90 degrees
Break over at C2 and/or C3 or 4	Poll high, smooth curved neck
Open mouth	Closed relaxed mouth
Sores in mouth & tongue	Confidence to the hand
Tongue high or sticking out	Quiet chewing of the bit
TMJ dysfunction	Comfortable jaw
Rigidity of movement	Undulating fluid movement
Extensions with knee straight	Extensions with slight knee flex
Conformation appears faulty	Conformation is enhanced

We have seen so many "competitively" trained horses that few people recognize the lack of classical training. When showing, even the judges seem to be picking the over flexed horses even though it clearly states in classical training manuals and in USDF regulations that the poll should be the highest point and between 80 to 90 degrees flexion. The trot and its extensions are picked on the natural talent of the horse for big movement even though it is trailing, rather than in correct carriage with weight brought properly under. We need a world-wide effort to make dressage fans more and more knowledgeable of the results of correct training results so that proper training is required. This should give our horses much relief from the rapidly growing need for care due to pain and overuse injuries.